Outsmarting the Scam Artists

Outsmarting the Scam Artists

How to Protect Yourself From the Most Clever Cons

WITHDRAWN

Doug Shadel

WILEY

John Wiley & Sons, Inc.

Published by John Wiley & Sons, Inc., Hoboken, New Jersey.
Published simultaneously in Canada.

No part of this publication may be reproduced, stored in a retrieval system, or transmitted in any form or by any means, electronic, mechanical, photocopying, recording, scanning, or otherwise, except as permitted under Section 107 or 108 of the 1976 United States Copyright Act, without either the prior written permission of the Publisher, or authorization through payment of the appropriate per-copy fee to the Copyright Clearance Center, Inc., 222 Rosewood Drive, Danvers, MA 01923, (978) 750-8400, fax (978) 646-8600, or on the Web at www.copyright.com. Requests to the Publisher for permission should be addressed to the Permissions Department, John Wiley & Sons, Inc., 111 River Street, Hoboken, NJ 07030, (201) 748-6011, fax (201) 748-6008, or online at www.wiley.com/go/permissions.

Limit of Liability/Disclaimer of Warranty: While the publisher and author have used their best efforts in preparing this book, they make no representations or warranties with respect to the accuracy or completeness of the contents of this book and specifically disclaim any implied warranties of merchantability or fitness for a particular purpose. No warranty may be created or extended by sales representatives or written sales materials. The advice and strategies contained herein may not be suitable for your situation. You should consult with a professional where appropriate. Neither the publisher nor author shall be liable for any loss of profit or any other commercial damages, including but not limited to special, incidental, consequential, or other damages.

For general information on our other products and services or for technical support, please contact our Customer Care Department within the United States at (800) 762-2974, outside the United States at (317) 572-3993, or fax (317) 572-4002.

Wiley also publishes its books in a variety of electronic formats. Some content that appears in print may not be available in electronic books. For more information about Wiley products, visit our web site at www.wiley.com.

This and other AARP books are available at AARP's online bookstore, aarp.org/bookstore.

Library of Congress Cataloging-in-Publication Data:

Shadel, Doug, 1957–
    Outsmarting the scam artists : how to protect yourself from the most clever cons / Doug Shadel.
        p.   cm.
    Includes bibliographical references and index.
    ISBN 978-1-118-17364-0 (pbk.); 978-1-118-22702-2 (ebk); 978-1-118-24007-6 (ebk); 978-1-118-26467-6 (ebk)
        1. Fraud–Prevention.   2. Swindlers and swindling.   I. Title.
    HV6691.S42   2012
    613.6—dc23
                                                                2011050802

Printed in the United States of America
10 9 8 7 6 5 4 3 2 1

This book is dedicated to the hundreds
of public servants and volunteers who
have devoted their lives to fighting fraud
in all its forms.

Contents

Contents

Part III   How to Fight Fraud

Acknowledgments

I would like to thank the following individuals for their contributions, directly or indirectly, to this book: Scott Adkins; Emily Allen; Lona Choi-Allum; John Barnett; Crystal Tolbert Bell; Dan Bolick; Joe Borg; Alan Buie; Elliot Burg; Bruce Carlson; Kathi Brown; Laura Carstensen; Pat Cashman; Rachelle Cummins; Martha Deevy; Shari Delaney; Jimmy Edwards; Rob Ence; Jason Erskine; John Gannon; Lois Greisman; Chuck Harwood; Bill Hessle; Kathryn Holguin; Sally Hurme; Christine Kieffer; Melodye Kleinman; Dan Lord; Erin Leahy; Jodi Lipson; Ellyn Lindsey; Shoshana Lucich; Jean Mathisen; Greg Marchildon; Ingrid McDonald; Rob McKenna; Amy Nofziger; Nanna Notthoff; Karla Pak; Anthony Pratkanis; Jennifer Sauer; Susanne Schiebe; Lori Schock; Mike Schuster; Emily, Nick, and Renee Shadel; Bridget Small; Chris Raaum; John Risjman; Terri Thome; Doug Walsh; Gerri Walsh; Cheryl Weber; and Lee White.

PREFACE

The Big Myth about Fraud

Anyone who has spent time giving talks in the community about how to avoid fraud encounters a common reaction: "This is all well and good for other people, but I'm too smart to ever fall for one of these scams."

People who make such comments haven't met Dave Benson, a highly successful businessman who retired in 2002 with a nest egg of more than $2 million dollars. Two years later, he had lost nearly $650,000 of it to an oil and gas scam out of Dallas, Texas.

They also haven't met Steve Johnson, a 20-year veteran stockbroker who got to age 58 and saw that his 401(k) was not sufficient to pay for his retirement, so he started investing in high-risk investments like rare stamps, stock options, and oil and gas units. He eventually lost $75,000.

And then there was Allen Jennings, a college professor at the University of California with a PhD in organic chemistry who lost $800,000 to a series of movie scam investments operating out of Hollywood, California.

The list goes on. Research conducted by AARP and the Financial Industry Regulatory Authority (FINRA) Foundation found that investment fraud victims had more education, earned more, and were more financially literate than the general population. Many victim lists look like a who's who of American business.

So why are so many people in denial about their own susceptibility to this crime? Part of it is human nature. Health psychologists long ago identified something known as "the illusion of invulnerability."

This is the human tendency to under estimate one's own chance of getting a serious illness and it is a major barrier to changing one's behavior. For if a person thinks, as apparently many do, that "other people get cancer, but I won't," they will never take any steps to avoid it. The same illusion holds true for becoming a fraud victim. If you don't think you will be taken, you won't take steps to avoid it.

One goal of this volume is to convince the reader that anyone, no matter how intelligent or successful, can be taken given the right circumstances and the right con man. You will see numerous examples in these pages of extraordinarily sharp business people who fell prey to the sophisticated psychological tactics con men employ.

The New Frontier: Emotion and Persuasion

New research has uncovered the two primary tools con artists employ to defraud victims: heightened emotions and persuasion. With regard to emotions, the con artist's first order of business is to get the victim into a heightened emotional state known as "ether." The con artists all believe that heightened emotions make it easier to push the target into a poor decision because they are less able to access the thinking part of the brain and raise objections based on logic and reason. Social scientists have known for years that not only do we make poor decisions when we are in a heightened emotional state, but we are also notoriously poor at realizing how much influence such emotions have on our decisions. This suggests that fraud prevention efforts should include information about the impact of emotion on decision-making.

Another key tool employed by con artists is persuasion. Researchers have discovered that while new scams arise everyday, the underlying persuasion tactics employed in those scams remain fairly constant. They have also discovered that fraud victims are less able than the general public to spot persuasion tactics used by con men. Thus, an emerging new strategy in the fight against fraud is to teach people the persuasion tactics used in all scams. And as we describe in Chapter 13, there is growing evidence that such prevention tactics are effective.

Targeting Vulnerable Populations

An estimated 10 to 15 percent of the U.S. population falls for one kind of scam or another each year.[1] While theoretically anyone can be victimized, researchers have discovered that there are certain demographic, psychological, and behavioral characteristics that make some people more susceptible to fraud than others. This suggests that prevention messages can be targeted to particular vulnerable populations instead of having to reach everyone. For example, a 2011 study by the AARP Foundation found that the average fraud victim was 69 years old. Other studies of known victims have found the average victim age to range between 55 and 65 years old.[2] We discuss this new profiling research and how it is being applied in the field in Chapters 11 and 13.

Another important prevention tool, outlined in Chapter 3, is understanding the stages that con men take their victims through in a typical scam. This is simply another way for investors to be able to see a bad guy coming from a distance.

One final point about this book: The sources used to describe how fraud works are equal measures of social science research, law enforcement case files, victim profiles, and interviews with con artists. The insights from former con artists provide an unprecedented glimpse inside the mind of these swindlers. The 12 master cons quoted herein have collectively stolen hundreds of millions of dollars from American investors and consumers. Most of these cons insisted on hiding their identity, so we have given them each a pseudonym (see "Meet the Cons").

What are they saying? In reviewing hundreds of pages of interview transcripts with con artists over the years, the insights they have provided are remarkably consistent. You might say that the "findings" from these interviews have been replicated over and over. There is very little disagreement among cons about the basic tactics they employ.

This volume reveals nothing less than the scam artist's playbook, a detailed inventory of the strategies and tactics cons employ to defraud consumers. Our hope is that by understanding how these strategies and tactics work, we can begin to chip away at this pernicious social problem.

Meet the Cons

Rick Barnes—Barnes spent more than 15 years perpetrating one mail fraud scheme after another until his arrest and conviction in 2008. **Specialty: Lottery and prize fraud.**

Pete Chambers—Chambers was arrested in the mid-1990s as part of a massive sweep of fraudulent telemarketing rooms by the federal government. He served several years in federal prison for his crimes. **Specialty: Free prize/lottery scams.**

Jimmy Edwards—Edwards worked in more than 30 fraudulent boiler rooms mostly in south Florida between 1996 until his arrest in 2004. He was convicted of fraud and served 37 months in prison. **Specialty: Business opportunity scams.**

Mike Harris—Harris worked in oil-and-gas boiler rooms in Texas and Oklahoma for seven years in the 2000s. He was never charged with fraud but was named in lawsuits where victims sued firms in which he worked. **Specialty: Oil and gas scams.**

Chuck Jones—Jones worked in charity-fraud boiler rooms for several years before being arrested in 1995 along with 200 others in an FBI sweep of telemarketing rooms nationwide. **Specialty: Charity scams.**

Ed Joseph—Joseph worked for more than 20 years as an owner and operator of fraudulent boiler rooms across the country. **Specialty: Gold coins/investments.**

Ron Mann—Mann was co-founder and lead preacher of Globadine Ministries, the largest religious-based Ponzi scheme in U.S. history. Globadine took in more than $450 million in 10 years. **Specialty: Ponzi schemes.**

Sara Needleman—Needleman spent a decade as a meth addict and identity thief until her arrest and conviction in 2003. Her mother told her to tell AARP how she did it. **Specialty: Identity theft.**

Preface

Jeremy Shipman—Shipman worked in multiple fraudulent boiler rooms over the years before being convicted in 2009. He is currently serving a 33-month sentence in federal prison. **Specialty: Gold coins/investment scams.**

Freddy Smith—As far as we know, Smith has never been charged with a crime. He has trained hundreds of con men over the years on the craft of swindling people over the phone and has served as an informant for several law enforcement agencies. **Specialty: Investments/gold coin scams.**

Bill Sullivan—Sullivan owned and operated several fraudulent boiler rooms that raised money for low-cost Hollywood movies. He took in more than $20 million from 800 investors before being indicted by the U.S. Justice Department. Sullivan is currently serving a three-year jail sentence. **Specialty: Movie investment scams.**

Johnny Weber—Weber was a top closer of oil-and-gas deals in Texas. He was arrested after a firm he started took in $14 million in 18 months. Weber is currently serving a 10-year prison term. **Specialty: Oil-and-gas investments.**

PART

I

THE SCAM ARTISTS' PLAYBOOK

CHAPTER 1

Inside the Con Artist's Mind

Pay phone/internet rtes
$150,000/yr possible
Call 1-800-888-8888

Have you ever seen an ad like this and wondered what they were offering? This ad appeared in the *Baltimore Sun* and in newspapers around the country in October 1999. It is known in the scam boiler room world as a "blind ad" because it is hard to tell from reading it what they are selling. Regardless of what is being sold, the "$150,000/yr possible" claim generates thousands of phone calls and in this case, all the calls were going to a south Florida business called All American Pay Phones (not its real name).

While pay phones have gone the way of the eight-track cassette and may seem dated, the techniques used to scam people have not changed over time. Our expert con artists tell us that swindlers are selling smartphone distributorships today the same way they sold pay phones in the 1990s.

All American was one of the many firms that con artists like Jimmy Edwards worked for during the 1990s, and he is going to take us on a behind-the-scenes tour of that company. But before we do that, let's listen in on a call that came into All American in

November 1999 while Edwards was working there. The call was handled by one of his good friends and colleagues, Joe Vertega.

Vertega: Good afternoon, this is Joe. Can I help you?

Swanson: My name is John Swanson and I saw your ad in the paper about pay phones and I was calling to get more information.

Vertega: Great. What city and state are you calling from?

Swanson: Rockville, Maryland.

Vertega: OK. And how close is Rockville to Washington D.C.?

Swanson: About 25 minutes.

Vertega: Great because it looks like most of the lucrative locations that are available now will be in a large urbanized market like D.C., okay?

Swanson: Okay.

Vertega: And there is no one up and operating there currently. I have no vendors in that market, John. We're just moving into it, and it looks like it is up for grabs. Are you interested in starting a small business for yourself?

Swanson: I am. I really am interested.

Vertega: Do you have any background in the pay phone business?

Swanson: No, not really.

Vertega: Have you ever used a pay phone in the past?

Swanson: Yes.

Vertega: Well then, you're qualified, okay?

This dialogue is typical of the first interaction one has with a business-opportunity firm like All American. The operator transfers callers to one of 8 to 10 salesmen who will then proceed to sell you on receiving a packet of information about pay phone distributorships.

The particular conversation you are "listening" to is a transcript of an undercover tape recording made by the Federal Trade Commission in 1999.[1] John Swanson is really an undercover investigator setting up the company to gather evidence against them for suspected business-opportunity fraud. Joe Vertega is one of All American's best salespeople. Let's keep listening.

> Vertega: Pay phones are a very simple business, you understand. They've been around over 80-something years, okay? It doesn't take a rocket scientist to pull quarters out of a pay phone.
>
> All American is the largest privately owned pay phone distributor in the United States today. We've got almost 4,000 active vendors on the rosters now all across the continental United States. I'm also moving into southwest Canada, I'm into Alaska, Hawaii, the U.S. Virgin Islands. I'm also into Puerto Rico now. And here I sit in our corporate offices in Miami.

From the description of the company offered by Mr. Vertega, one might get the impression that All American was a large corporation with hundreds of white collar workers bustling around the office servicing clients throughout the continental United States. And from the confident sound of his voice, one might also conclude that Mr. Vertega was a successful Miami businessman who was simply trying to expand his already thriving pay phone distributor business.

Both of these impressions would be wrong.

Miami, Florida, in the late 1990s looked like any other large U.S. city. But if you had the right tour guide and were able to look inside its many commercial office buildings, you would find every kind of fraudulent boiler room ever invented: oil and gas rooms, vending machine rooms, Internet kiosk rooms, prepaid cell phone rooms, prepaid legal rooms, prepaid pornography rooms, gold coin rooms, online casino gambling rooms. You name the scam, there was a room that operated that scam.

From 1996 until 2004, Jimmy Edwards worked in them all: more than 30 different fraudulent boiler rooms in Miami. It was the heyday of business-opportunity fraud, Edward's personal specialty, but he would work in any room that paid well.

"I jumped from room to room during that time—cause hey you gotta put food on the table," recalls Edwards. "There were a lot of characters running in and out of those rooms." The room with the most characters was All American.

In 1999, Edwards had just gotten out of rehab for heroin addiction and was looking for a room that was a little loose in terms of the pressure they would put on him to perform right away. He was recruited to go to work for All American by its manager Jeremy when he was at a Narcotics Anonymous (N.A.) meeting. It turns out that boiler room owners regularly sent managers in to N.A. meetings to recruit addicts to work at their rooms. Why?

> Who better to get on the phone than an addict? Nobody. Who's a better talker than an addict? Nobody. Who has more motivation for money than an addict? Nobody. I was an addict from New York and I knew how to hustle. So they were falling all over themselves to get me on the phone when they were first introduced to me down there.

So while Mr. Vertega might have sounded authoritative in proclaiming All American to be the largest private pay phone distributor in the continental United States, the reality was quite different. Consider Edwards' rundown of the All American staff roster:

> All American was a room full of drug addicts. Jeremy the manager was a crack head. He's the one who recruited me at the N.A. meeting. He could barely go a week without going on a run and smoking $2,000 to $3,000 worth of crack, winding up in a hotel room somewhere with us having to go find him or sending somebody out to pull him out of the hotel room, get him cleaned up, and get him back into his seat as a manager. So with him as our fearless leader, imagine what the room was like.
>
> We had Rick. He was from Hoboken, New Jersey, and he was a crack head too. Same type of crack head as Jeremy. He knew the pay phone business and he had a little rhythm. He was a decent closer.
>
> Then there was Dave. He was a helluva addict too. Dave was a Jewish kid, clean cut, lived with his mother. He was older than me so he was probably in his late 30s, early 40s back then. He was a loner.
>
> Jack was another one. Big J would go out on a Friday with $10,000 and we'd have to go pick him up Monday morning

and he had no shoes on in an open locker somewhere . . . broke, broke, broke, 10Gs gone, no shirt, no shoes, standing at a pay phone, 11 o'clock in the morning on Monday. Blown out—he smoked $10,000 worth of crack. Ten thousand dollars worth of crack and hookers and cabs and pipes and everything else that comes with what you are doing when you are smoking crack in a hotel room . . . he'd go through every penny.

Then there was Karl. Karl was a dope shooter like me. And he and I used to team up. You know with heroin, if you don't have any when you wake up in the morning, you're not in good shape. You need what's called "a wake up." Most heroin addicts will try to save something from the night before for when they wake up. But most heroin addicts can't. So what happens is we would get to the office and try to get money together to go buy dope so we could get straight.

Jeremy, the manager, always had money and he knew what we needed, so he would spot me and Karl $100 for $150 back on Thursday. Karl would take that $100 and fly down to Overtown on his motorcycle and he'd buy 10 bags. Then when he came back, we would go into the bathroom and we would set up and shoot up, get straight, and go back in the room—reinvented, two completely new people. And then we would get on the phone, calling all our old paper and doing our thing.

Other guys would do the same thing with crack. They'd go into the bathroom and smoke crack. And they'd come back in and be all steamed up with their eyes bulging out of their heads. But they were able to get on the phone and pitch people on the phone deal.

And what about this guy Joe Vertega? Vertega, as it turns out, was the most interesting character of them all.

Joe was a nice guy but for sure a crack head. You gotta understand something. This is a guy who is about 240 to 245 pounds, 6 foot 3. As soon as he got a hit of crack in him, off came his clothes, on went a dress, high heels, and blue eye makeup and off to the boulevard he went, turning tricks. And this is a guy who had pockets full of money, because he was so good at closing deals. It was just what he did. Another aspect of his addiction, you know?

So evidently there was more to Mr. Vertega than his deep knowledge of the pay phone distributor business. Let's hear some more of his presentation:

> Vertega: Now John, you'll be guaranteed to earn no less than $300 per phone. Per month. That is in writing. Now how is that for a safety net? So we expect you to recover your initial investment between the first seven to nine months. One hundred percent return. If I brought you in as an entry level with seven of the new generation smart phones, you're looking at approximately a $15,000 overall investment. Are you capable of dealing with that?

> Swanson: Yes I am.

> Vertega: That's not a problem for you? Okay. So we're on the same page with one another and you understand I just have to be sure. We take 300 plus calls a week here, John. I hope you understand the number of flakes and nuts I talk to, sir.

What Vertega is doing in this part of the pitch is "qualifying the money"—making sure the potential victim has the $15,000 to spend before he goes any further with him. The irony is that Vertega was demanding that the customer prove to him that he was not one of the "flakes and nuts" who called All American every week . . . just before he went into the bathroom to smoke some crack and dress up in high heels, blue eye make-up, and a dress to go turn tricks on Biscayne Boulevard. We will check in on the rest of this presentation in Chapter 8.

Edwards says that not everyone in the boiler rooms he worked in had such severe drug addiction going on, but almost all of them had some kind of addiction. "I would say 80 to 90 percent of the people I worked with in these boiler rooms were addicted to something: alcohol, pot, barbiturates, coke, heroin. It just kind of came with the territory."

Despite the prevalence of drug and alcohol addiction, most fraud boiler room salespeople came from decent backgrounds. As Edwards explains it, if you have had no exposure to the life of wealth and comfort, it is impossible to fake it and therefore impossible to persuade people with money to hand it over.

> Closers aren't like down in the gutter junkies who come from complete devastation. They have to have been exposed to some structure, some type of educated people with scruples during their developmental years in order to have some of the mental skills necessary to be a closer.

Neal Shover, a noted sociologist who has written about white collar crime, conducted a study in 2004 of 47 federal inmates who had all worked in fraudulent boiler rooms. He reaches a similar conclusion about where these cons come from.

> In stark contrast to those of street criminals, the telemarketers we interviewed typically described the financial circumstances in their parental homes as secure if not comfortable and their parents as conventional and hard working . . . A striking 68 percent (of their fathers) were business owners or held managerial positions. Consequently, a substantial proportion of the men and women were exposed to entrepreneurial perspectives and understandings while young.[2]

Edwards falls into this same category. "My mother and father are married 57 years after all. I have three sisters; I was the baby in a stable Italian family who became a drug addict. I was the black sheep of the family."

This has also been the experience of AARP researchers' interviews with con men over the years. Many of them have been like Edwards, with relatively stable backgrounds and ambitious, business-oriented family members. But many cons also report being heavy drug and alcohol users while they were scamming people. Criminologists have long since established a link between drug use, criminal behavior, and low self-control.

No Conscience

If drugs and alcohol were a constant presence in fraud boiler rooms, there was clearly one thing missing: conscience. One of the most extreme examples of this lack of conscience was a deal Edwards did at All American with his friend Jack.

Jack was on the phone pitching a couple in Missouri, and they wanted 25 phones. But Jack kept hearing this odd sucking sound on the other end of the phone. And he finally says, "Excuse me John. What is that noise?" And the guy says, "Well me and my wife are paraplegics. That is why we are looking for something like this. We want to be able to hire somebody who can be our hands and feet. We can take the money that we won from the accident and invest in something and have one employee and supervise him, drive him around to the locations to maintain the phones, clean them out, take the money and the coins and we will do all the paperwork, keep track of everything, and pay him as an employee."

It was apparently not unusual to have a disabled person on the phone, so Jack had no problem going for the close. But the guy was hard to nail down. He wasn't saying no, but he wasn't saying yes. So Jack told him he should come down for a fly and buy. He said, "Listen John, here is what I want you to do. You want 25 phones but you are a little apprehensive, a little uncomfortable. I don't blame ya. Why don't you do this: book a flight and fly on down here and kick the wastepaper basket, make sure it's full of paper, look at me—you'll see I'm as real as your right arm, take a walk through the office, look at some phones, pick one up and use one, and get yourself feeling warm and fuzzy before we go any further with this thing. That is the most important thing in the world to me. Come on down. I tell you what I'll do. If you purchase, I'll knock the price of your flight and your hotel off the price of the deal. I'll pick it up myself. Fair enough?"

The guy finally said to Jack, "Well you know Jack, I think I'm going to take you up on that fly and buy, but I'm going to drive." And 48 hours later, 9 o'clock in the morning, I come into the office and there are two wheel chairs in the lobby. Guy's got the thing you blow on . . . that's how ill he was. I could not believe it. I walked in and looked at Jack and he looked at me and as cynical as we were then, we almost fell on the floor laughing hysterically at this whole thing. And sure enough, Jack closed him. They left him with a check for $72,000. We sold $5,000 worth of pay phones for $72,000 to two paraplegics in wheel chairs and laughed all the way to the bank. I know it's terrible, and I am ashamed now that I actually found that amusing at that time.

Creating a Persona

Edward's description of the drug culture in fraud boiler rooms has been confirmed both by academic studies and our own interviews with more than a dozen con men over the years. The culture of the rooms seems to be characterized by fast money, fast women, drug binges, alcohol, and lots of lying and cheating among employees. So how do these obviously dysfunctional business operations manage to look legitimate and convince a wide range of people to turn over their money? One of the key strategies con men employ is to develop a "persona" that makes them look legitimate and helps convince victims to part with their money. In the world of cons and frauds, there are two types of personas: individual and corporate.

Individual Persona

An individual persona is a character that you build up in your head and whose identity you assume before you get on the phone. Edwards said it was a basic part of the training he conducted with new fraud salespeople.

> I'd say picture yourself behind the big mahogany desk, with the credenza, with the big office, the family portrait on the desk, your telephone, your autographed football and jerseys hanging on the wall, the pool table on the left hand side. You are this bigwig that everybody is waiting to talk to. The whole idea is when you get down to asking for the money, you can't show one lick of fear or hesitation or doubt that this isn't hands

down the greatest decision this client on the other end of the phone is making for their lives and for their family and for their future. Period the end.

Con artists will build personas around their own personal style of pitching. Edward's style was to act like the big shot in the building and so he would never chase a deal.

Some guys were just relentless in brow-beating a client until they finally gave in. I would never do that. The reason I wouldn't do it is because my persona was to be this top executive. Would Donald Trump beg a customer or brow-beat someone to get a lousy $15,000 to $20,000 check? No. Would Bill Gates? Of course not. So neither would Jimmy Edwards, super closer. I walked away from a lot of deals when the mark was jacking me around, but it was worth it to keep the persona intact.

Several years ago, an informant provided us with training tapes being used to train boiler room salespeople in what was at the time one of the biggest fraudulent operations in the United States. The training tapes had lots of examples of how to cold call people and also emphasized the same thing our con artists emphasize. You have to build up a confident persona so that you can appear successful even if you are not. They give the trainees instructions to write down as specifically as they can exactly who they are (or who they would like to be) when they are on the phone: How much income they make, who their clients are, how long they have been in the business, how successful they have been. And then they tell them to post that description near the phone so they will constantly be reminded of this created personality that will breathe confidence into them when they are going through the inevitable rejection of calling 200 people a day and getting hung up on 150 of those 200 times.

Mike Harris, who worked in fraudulent oil and gas boiler rooms for nearly a decade, said it was a real macho culture. "You absolutely had to have that swagger, that supreme confidence to cold call a doctor or a big-time lawyer and sound as though you were an oil company

Pioneers of Fraud: Bertha Heyman

Bertha Heyman, otherwise known as "Big Bertha" or "The Confidence Queen," was a master swindler who operated in the 1870s and 1880s. Heyman was an early innovator in the art of establishing a false persona, which she used to induce wealthy victims to loan her money. Despite her homely appearance and heavy frame (5'4", 250 pounds), Heyman was able to assume the identity of a wealthy heiress who had just inherited millions of dollars.

Bertha Heyman, master swindler who operated in the 1870s and 1880s

Heyman stayed at all the finest hotels and was accompanied by an entourage of servants. She even had a personal physician and wore only the finest clothes to complete the picture of wealthy heiress.

In one of the earliest forms of advance fee scheme, she would typically approach a victim, describe in great detail all the wealthy people she knew and the vast sums she was about to inherit, then explain the need for short term cash in exchange for vast returns of interest later—which of course never arrived.

One news story described her writing letters while in prison to a victim to ask for money so she could bribe the warden to give her better accommodations. She denied bribing the warden, but did admit to writing the letters. When asked why she did it, she boldly replied:

> I am a swindler as you know and I wrote those letters because it suited my purpose. I lied in them. If it should suit my convenience tomorrow to tell you another story, I should do so.[3]

In another news article in the 1880s, she was quoted as saying:

> I take no pride in overvailing a fool. The moment I discover a man's a fool, I let him drop. But I delight in getting into the confidence and pockets of men who think they can't be "skinned." It ministers to my intellectual pride.[4]

executive. And what made it especially tough was that we were calling hundreds of people a day and getting hung up on most of the time."

■ ■ ■

Another con man who used a particular persona was Ed Joseph. Joseph, unlike Edwards, was one of those closers who would just brow-beat the target to death. In one gold coin pitch, the target of his pitch said "no" to him 55 times, yet he was absolutely relentless in his resolve to get the guy to say yes. "I used this conversation as a training tape to show new guys that persistence pays off. But you also learn to pick up on little clues the victim gives you that even though they are saying no, they really mean yes."

Joseph was an interesting figure because unlike so many of the other con artists we have interviewed, he was never a drug addict. This may explain why he lasted more than 20 years in the fraud business before finally being arrested in 1998. Joseph was particularly gifted at using his ability to entertain people on the phone at the same time that he was brow-beating them into compliance: "Mr. Jones, if you can't make up your mind, I will make it up for you. That is what I do here."

But the con man who took the artificial sales persona the furthest was a telemarketer named Pete Chambers. We interviewed Chambers in a jail cell in 1997 after the FBI take down of more than 200 salesmen across the nation. Pete used to employ different voices to give the impression that his operation was bigger and more established than it really was. So for instance, near the end of his scam career, Pete was making calls from a cell phone in a hotel room using three distinct voices, beginning with his own:

> (Telemarketer voice)—Sir, My name is Pete Chambers. Congratulations, you have walked away with one of the biggest awards we have ever given away. A $100,000 cashier's check. Congratulations to you. Now I want you to hold the line for just a moment, the Executive Vice President of the company, Charlie Miller, wants to personally congratulate you. Now I want you to hold on. I'm a little nervous because he's my boss. Hold the line, ok?

(Authoritative Voice) Mr. Jones, Charlie Miller here. How are you? I want to extend a warm and hearty congratulations to you on behalf of my entire staff. Congratulations to you.

(Telemarketer Voice)—Mr. Jones, Pete Chambers here again, boy that was my boss and I'm a little nervous, but again, when he comes in the room and congratulates you, you know you have done well for yourself. Now I need you to hold the line for just one second, I need to get my photographer, Mr. Robert Jones, on the phone. Hold the line.

(Informal/Southern accent) Mr. Jones, my last name is Jones too—I am Mr. Robert Jones from Mobile, Alabama. I'll be coming out your house personally to take photographs of ya. Congratulations!

Chambers pulled off the ultimate manipulation of persona when he managed to con a person out of $20,000 while he was in custody at a Las Vegas prison. He went out to use the pay phone and then called a victim, told him he was doing his weekend warrior duty as a United States Marshall down at the jail and needed him to go to the bank, withdraw $20,000 and wire it to a third party, a request the victim apparently complied with.

Corporate Persona

The idea behind developing a distinct persona is to present oneself with supreme confidence and increase one's chances of getting the sale. Another benefit of a well-established persona is to increase what persuasion experts call *source credibility*.[5] This is the notion that we are much more likely to do business with people who are well-established and credible.

To create the corporate persona, many con men spend a fortune on the external trappings of success, everything from fancy cars to expensive jewelry to plush office space, and even yachts. They will do anything they have to do to reinforce the impression that the operation and the person you are talking to is successful.

Bill Sullivan was convicted in 2009 of running a fraudulent movie deal boiler room. In the end, he took in more than

$20 million dollars from 800 investors and spent much of that money on the trappings of success. We interviewed Sullivan in 2009 just before he went to federal prison. "I was pitching the fast and glamorous Hollywood life, so that meant I had to have the million-dollar Malibu home, the Hummer limo," he told us. "We would routinely fly investors in from the Midwest to meet the stars in our next movie. It was all about creating the look of success." Unfortunately for Bill and for his investors, what started out as a desire to look impressive and wealthy led to gross over-expenditures, lavish self-indulgence, and ultimately bankruptcy and a federal fraud conviction.

Edwards said the first thing they did when starting up a new scam operation was to create a fancy-looking web site with testimonials from customers and glowing news articles about their hot new industry.

"One of the things that enhanced our corporate persona was advertising on big time radio and TV stations," said Edwards. "And then we went really crazy and started hiring big name actors to do TV spots for us on those channels. That really got the phones ringing."

The trouble was of course that these big time movie stars had no idea what they were promoting. They just wanted the work. As Bill Sullivan said, "Once we realized we could get an actual movie star for $50,000 for a day and fly investors in to meet them, we had it made. Lots of times these stars weren't even in the movies we were making, but they would spend the day on our set anyway because they were on the clock."

Conclusion

If there is anything to be learned from the example of All American Pay Phones it is this: Things are not always as they appear to be. All American appeared from the outside to be a legitimate business opportunity in the private pay phone business. It operated in a professional-looking office suite in Miami, spent hundreds of thousands of dollars on display advertising, and had glossy brochures describing the "smart" pay phones. Joe Vertega had a strong, confident voice and an encyclopedic command of the details of the business.

The only problem was that All American Pay Phone was a scam and everyone working there was actively trying to defraud as many people as possible. The Federal Trade Commission (FTC) took them down in 2000 for violating multiple state and federal laws. When All American went down, all the drug-addicted salesmen in the room scattered with the wind. But the wind didn't blow them too far. According to Edwards, almost all of the All American phone salesmen simply moved either across the street or in some cases, just up one or two floors in the same building to begin working in their next "business opportunity."

The con's ability to create false personas of themselves and the companies they work for and move around whenever they are discovered are keys to success in the fraud business. The last thing firms like All American want is to look like who they really are: a bunch of con artists trolling for easy money. Precisely how they pull off these illusions and why we fall for them is the subject of the rest of this volume.

CHAPTER 2

Ether

The Con Artist's Central Strategy

The crush or the kill is emotionally driven. It's not logic. If you apply logic to this concept, it's no. I am not going to send you my hard-earned money. I don't even know who you are. I don't know you from Adam.

—Jimmy Edwards, former con man

There are many elements to the fraud game, including hundreds of different persuasion tactics employed by clever con artists like the ones you met in Chapter 1. We will be describing many of these tactics in later chapters. But years of research and interviews with numerous con artists have revealed a remarkably consistent finding. The single most important strategy all con artists employ is to get the victim "under the ether."

Ether is con-artist slang for a heightened emotional state that causes the victim to react emotionally instead of thinking logically. It is that fuzzy haze we humans experience when we are overly excited about something and our visceral emotions swamp our ability to think rationally. Remember the first time you fell in love or a time when someone cut you off on the highway and you were seething with anger for hours. As we have seen from Chapter 1, con artists know this terrain well. After all, drug addiction is all about living in the moment and bouncing from one drug-induced emotional impulse to another in search of the next fix.

In this chapter, we will hear directly from former con artists who describe the role of ether in practicing their craft. We will also describe an example of what can happen when one makes major financial decisions while under the ether. Finally, we will review some of the science that explains why making decisions "under the ether" can lead to poor decisions and ultimately victimization.

What Con Artists Say about Ether

Edwards describes the role of heightened emotions in pitching victims: "Emotion is unpredictable. It peaks and valleys. And once you know where to take the person for the peak, and you can keep them up in that altitude, then you can control them. If you drop them back into the valley of logic, you're gonna lose them."

We will see several examples in later chapters of precisely how Edwards and others execute this strategy of finding and pushing the victim's emotional buttons to induce ether.

But Edwards isn't the only one of our con men who says emotion is the key to creating vulnerability. "Freddy" is a frenetically nervous former con man based in Los Angeles who trained hundreds of other fraudulent telemarketers over the years. He believes emotion is the only thing that makes victims vulnerable to scams. And just listening to him makes one begin to get a sense of how these con artists can ratchet up nervous energy:

> You're excited, you're excited, you're excited. Your adrenaline is up. You want to make money. You're my guy. It's on. We're going to the moon. Train has left. I got you the best seat on the train. Let's roll. You're going to brag to your golf buddies at the golf course on the third hole. You're in the ether.

Freddy is also quick to point out how different investments have different emotions: "Every investment has an emotion to it. Oil and gas has an emotion. Movies have an emotion. Gold has an emotion. In the early 1980s, gold hit $865 and it was a fever. It was a roaring bull market. And the experience was exhilarating. It was a compelling story that sold itself. The story was this: oil, international calamity, global unrest. The safe haven is gold. And the train is leaving. Get on it or you'll be sitting there while other people make fortunes. You can just hear the excitement building on the other end of that phone."

Bill Sullivan describes the emotion of movies: "There is no logical reason to invest in a movie deal. The big studios make all the money. It's all emotional. This is an emotional business. You're buying an emotion. You're not buying on logic. You're not buying on fact. You're buying off a glossy sheet of a brochure that was printed two weeks prior by some creative artist person showing, you know, the Hollywood sign."

Like Freddy, Bill says the key is excitement: "If you own a widget company in Iowa and you're making a million dollars a year and you've been doing this for 20 years, and your dad did it before you, you're kind of bored. You're making money but you've got it under control. If I can get you emotionally involved in being able to be a part of a Hollywood movie, where you get to come down to the set and have lunch with the stars, you are going to get excited and feel emotionally satisfied. You're going to feel the thrill, the challenge and once you buy my story, you're going to pretty much jump in both feet first. Once I emotionally connect with the investor, he closes himself."

Ed Joseph had this to say about the role of emotion in fraud: "I've heard this phrase, if it sounds too good to be true, it probably is. And that's the little voice inside of us, that's the warning signal that's going off and it's telling us, hey, this is something you should stay away from. But we don't listen to that little voice inside because our emotions are now in control and we're not thinking logically, we're not thinking reasonably."

This comment might explain in part why surveys done by AARP in the mid-1990s found that victims of fraud could parrot back prevention warnings like, "If it sounds too good to be true, it probably is" yet they were still defrauded.[1]

Joseph takes the role of emotion in decision-making a step further: "I've learned that most of us base our decisions in life on our emotions and then we try to justify our decisions with the facts. We like to think it's the other way around, but it's not. Take the car you buy. You probably decided to buy that Mercedes based on emotion, but in telling your wife why you drive a Mercedes, you don't tell her the real reason; you tell her about safety, you tell her about mileage, you tell her about dependability. You don't tell her that it's going to make you look so much more attractive to the ladies to drive a Mercedes."

This observation by a con man who dropped out of high school was echoed by one of the leading behavioral scientists on the role of affect on decision making. In a landmark article in 1980 on the topic, Robert Zajonc not only makes the same point as Joseph, but uses the same example: "We sometimes delude ourselves that we proceed in a rational manner and weigh all the pros and cons of the various alternatives. But this is probably seldom the actual case. Quite often 'I decided in favor of X' is no more than 'I liked X' . . . We buy the cars we 'like,' choose the jobs and houses we find 'attractive,' and then justify these choices by various reasons."[2]

Johnny Weber went so far as to take his victims to strip clubs where the entire atmosphere reeked of visceral emotion. "I can't tell you how may deals I got signed in clubs. You get these good ole boys a couple drinks, they start looking at the ladies and bragging about how much money they have. They ain't interested in reading the paperwork. They're interested in bragging to friends about being JR Ewing."

One of the clearest examples of the use of ether in fraud can be found in faith-based scams like the one we profile in Chapter 5, Globadine Ministries. Nothing engages the heart more quickly than religious worship, and the Globadine Ministries sales pitch was always preceded by at least 45 to 50 minutes of passionate songs of praise and worship in order to induce ether.

Edwards says that emotion is an invaluable sales tool because there are so many different kinds of emotion to choose from. "Most sales people focus on getting the person excited and chasing the money, which does work. But master closers realize there is a whole range of emotions that can be used. Believe it or not, some of my best sales came from unhappy customers calling me to scream and yell about how they were lied to about the product. I would let them vent until they were blue in the face, then once they had worked themselves into the ether, I would close them. Emotion is emotion. Anger is just as good as excitement or fear."

Case Study: The Effects of Ether on a Smart Investor

Dave Benson was a partner in a successful Midwest trading company for 20 years. In 2006, he retired with a retirement fund of more than $2 million. By all accounts, Benson had led a successful life: Married for 30 years, two kids in college, a substantial nestegg and with it, the prospect of a comfortable retirement.

Six months after retiring, Benson was contacted by a man selling oil and gas interests out of Dallas, Texas. While he was initially hesitant, the salesman gave him several references including the name of a prominent law firm that Benson was familiar with and the names of other investors who had purchased units and were pleased with the results. The returns promised to him were phenomenal: 80 to 100 percent the first year and after that—who knows? The sky is the limit.

Benson began by purchasing one unit for $150,000, but the salesmen kept calling and asking for more money and so Dave bought another unit. At one point, he realized he was not acting entirely rationally, so he actually put a post-it note on his phone that said, "Don't buy any more until the first investment pays off." But the salesmen told him this was going to set him and his family up for life and they only had a couple units left, so he kept buying. Over a three-month period, Dave purchased five units for a total investment of $650,000.

In the end, the investment turned out to be a scam, and Dave lost virtually all of his principal. He had been taken by salesmen from a boiler room not unlike the All American room described in Chapter 1.

When asked why he had invested so much with an oil and gas telemarketer, he said, "It was a combination of things. While I had retired with a decent nest egg, I always thought it could have been more if I had just done a better job of investing. I also felt kind of guilty about not spending more time with my two boys when they were younger. I wanted to leave them enough money so they would be set for life."

Tilling the Soil of Victimization

Two conditions are necessary to induce the ether state in a victim. First, there must be something about the victim's life situation that motivates him or her to want to engage with a salesman. It could be a financial need brought on by events like the loss of a job, an unanticipated medical expense, or the need to save more for retirement. Or it could be a psychological need like boredom, loneliness or, as was the case for Dave Benson, the need to leave a bigger inheritance for one's family.

The second condition is the con artist must be able to identify such emotional motivators and focus the victim's attention on them. In Dave's case, the salesman engaged him in several phone calls in which he probed for personal information and got Dave's whole back story about his feeling inadequate as an investor and—to some extent—as a father. This information was all the con man needed to put Dave under the ether and exploit him.

Is Dave the only high-powered investor who has fallen prey to such a ploy? Not by a long shot. Once he discovered the investment was a scam, Dave and a number of other investors sued the promoters and the case is pending. What is remarkable about his story and this case is that he found some 200 other victims of this scam whose average investment amount was more than $300,000 each! The occupations of these victims read like a Harvard University alumni newsletter: judges, business owners, medical doctors, deans of law schools, principals in major accounting firms, mega-farmers. It turns out that anyone can succumb to fraud in a vulnerable moment. The question is why.

What Social Science Teaches Us about Ether

The notion that a con artist would want to create vulnerability in victims by getting them to react emotionally is, well, logical. After all, what con artists are selling really only makes sense when one's thinking is clouded. The question is how does it work? What is going on in the brain that triggers us to react emotionally versus thinking an offer through? And why don't we seem to know when this is happening to be able to stop it?

Scientists generally believe that much of human behavior can be explained by the interaction of two different systems in the brain: the emotional or affective system and the rational or thinking system. While there is much debate over precisely how these systems interact and which is dominant, there is agreement on their general characteristics.

The emotional system in the brain has been with humans since the beginning, some six million years ago. From an evolutionary standpoint, emotional regions of the brain were designed to help humans and other animals stay alive by allowing them to react quickly to threats from predators.[3]

The classic example of the emotional system in action is demonstrated when we are confronted by danger, like an approaching lion. The primitive, emotional part of the brain instantly says "run for your life," and you do. Decisions made as part of the emotional brain tend to be characterized as hot, fast, unconscious and responsive to short-term, urgent needs.[4] It is also not as precise as the thinking part of the brain, and so while it receives messages more quickly, they are crude and contain less information.

The rational or thinking system of the brain evolved more recently—within the past 150,000 years. This rational center is responsible for making decisions based on cold logic, reason, and data. It is the part of the brain that makes humans unique among all species in that it allows us to plan for the future, think about the big picture, delay gratification, and weigh facts and situations logically before moving forward.

How the Thinking and Feeling Brains Work Together

Scientists used to think that stimuli would come into the brain and travel first to the rational center. This area would then send information on to the emotional center to have it evaluated based on stored memories of similar events. In this way, the two systems worked together. That was the story for many years of how the brain processed information and it is still the way most information is processed.

In the mid 1990s, however, a neurologist named Joseph LeDoux discovered a narrow pathway of neurons (which he calls the "low road") that allows part of the information in stimuli to split off and go directly to the emotional center of the brain. This pathway allows the information to travel twice as quickly to the emotional center as it does to the rational center. Because it gets there faster, even though the information is incomplete, if the stimuli are strong enough, they can "hijack" the rest of the brain and cause it to react before the rational part has had a chance to evaluate the data.[5]

Emotional Hijacking Equals Ether

This hijacking of the brain is essentially what we believe con artists describe as getting the victim "under the ether." Con artists will present strong emotional stimuli to the victim in the hope that the information will travel the aptly named "low road" and flood the rational thinking part of the victim's brain. Such a transaction can happen in a flash, leaving even the most competent and intelligent investor momentarily vulnerable to fraud.

When Dave Benson looks back at his experience with the oil and gas con artists and scratches his head about why he did what he did, he may very well be describing just such a hijacking. And when he put the post it note on his phone saying, "Don't buy more until the first investment pays off," that may have been the rational system in his brain pleading with the emotional system to come to its senses.

The Hot-Cold Empathy Gap

The notion that we humans make poor decisions when we are in a heightened emotional state has been well established both by leading social scientists and by many different con artists. But there is one more important fact that impacts our vulnerability to emotion and fraud. And that is that we humans are also notoriously poor at recognizing when we are in such a state and how it affects our decision-making. In a classic article summarizing this point, George Lowenstein describes what he calls the "hot-cold empathy gap":

> People who are in "hot" (emotional) states tend to under-appreciate the extent to which their preferences and behavioral inclinations are influenced by their affective state; they typically believe that they are behaving more dispassionately than they actually are.[6]

Lowenstein goes on to say that underestimating the influence of emotion on decision-making causes people to be over-confident about their ability to control their own decisions. Thus, our vulnerability increases by virtue of not realizing how much heightened emotional states influence us. But the reverse is also true. Lowenstein points out that humans are also notoriously poor at predicting what it's like to be in a future hot state when they are not emotionally aroused:

> When one is not hungry, afraid, or in pain . . . it is difficult to imagine what it would feel like to experience one of these states, or to fully appreciate the motivational power such states could have over one's own behavior. Because people who are in "cold" states tend to underestimate the motivational force of their own future hot states, they often fail to take measures to avoid situations that will induce such states.[7]

This inability to fully grasp how emotion or "affect" influences our decision-making is crucial to understanding why fraud occurs. A common response by the general public to stories of people losing thousands of dollars to fraud is, "How could they have been so dumb?" Even victims who are interviewed after the fact criticize themselves for falling for what later seemed like such an obvious scam. This is because they are no longer inside the situation—no longer having their emotions manipulated and vulnerabilities exposed. The ether has worn off.

Edwards described the fall out that occurs when the ether has worn off. "When I was selling business-opportunity scams, 40 to

50 percent of my customers would call back within a week and want to cancel—that's because the ether had worn off and they woke up one day and realized what they had done."

Precisely how do con artists induce such heightened emotional states that lead to victimization? And what can consumers and investors do to identify and resist it? These are the questions that will be addressed in the next several chapters.

The Stages of Fraud

Most fraud pitches come down to a simple formula:
front-drive-close.
> —Bill Sullivan, former investment-fraud promoter

Now that we have described the con artist's central strategy to put the victims into a heightened emotional state, we will look at the typical stages con artists take their victims through. For just as inflaming a potential victim's emotions is a common fraud strategy, there is also a fairly predictable sequence to the fraud game, particularly when it comes to business-opportunity and investment scams. By better understanding the stages of fraud, consumers will be better able to see such attempts coming and avoid victimization.

The primary source of our understanding of these stages is from the con artists that execute them. According to these experts, there are four main stages to the fraud game: the front, the drive, the close, and the load.

Stage One—The Front

Fronting means being the front of the operation—the person who first talks to the potential victim. The fronter's job is threefold: cast the net to see who might be interested, get the person excited with the prospect of phantom riches, and qualify the victim by making sure he or she has money.

Really skilled fronters will also profile the individual by gathering personal information to facilitate the onset of ether.

Casting the Net

The fronter in a boiler room is the person responsible for casting the net across the land to see who can be caught. There are many ways to cast the net, but a common one is to purchase lists of names called lead lists. Fronters then call 150 to 200 names a day from these lead sheets, hoping to deliver the complete pitch to at least 15 to 20 of the people they call. Of the 15 to 20 prospects the fronter may pitch, only two to four of them may agree to receive a packet containing all of the information about the opportunity. Interviews conducted with these fronters suggest that it is a tedious activity that results in a lot of hang-ups or emphatic "no" responses. This is one reason boiler room owners encourage telemarketers to develop the strong, confident persona described in Chapter 1.

Lead sheets used by these boiler rooms are acquired from lead brokers. One way that lead brokers get names of investors is by compiling names of people who have attended investment seminars or investment fairs or purchased particular types of high-risk investments in the past. By attending investment seminars or trade shows or dropping a business card off at a booth, you are sending a message that you are someone who is motivated to invest, which makes you more likely to say yes when the fronter calls on the phone.

Another way that boiler rooms get lead sheets is by buying, selling, or even stealing the names of other boiler rooms' customers. One con man we interviewed said the guy who ran his room would hire an attractive young woman to go to work for a competing boiler room. When the competitors weren't looking, she would steal the client list and deliver it to her real employer. And they say there is honor among thieves.

Boiler rooms also advertise in newspapers and on radio and television to induce interested investors to call. It is the fronter who answers those calls. Ed Joseph ran gold coin scams for years. He would routinely advertise on Christian radio stations. Why Christian radio? "Because their listeners believed in something that didn't exist and that's exactly what I was selling," Joseph said. Unsuspecting and naïve believers would call the scam operation, believing it was real because their favorite church station would never run scam advertising—or so they thought. He also said it was important that they call him, so that when they started objecting to the pitch, he could tell them, "Look buddy, you called me." This is an important control element that we will discuss later.

As we mentioned in Chapter 1, the boiler rooms Edwards worked in invested heavily in both print and TV advertising. When he was selling bogus Internet kiosks, the company was spending $150,000 per week advertising on television. "We had ads with famous actors in them and that gave us enough credibility to generate a lot of calls. At one time, we had 1,500 to 2,000 calls a day coming in," Joseph said.

Building Excitement with Phantom Riches

Whether the potential victims call in response to an ad or the fronter calls them, the first thing the fronter needs to do is get the person interested in the investment. This usually means using a persuasion tactic that researchers call *phantom riches*.[1] A phantom is something you desperately want, but which is normally unavailable. But the con artist is calling (or advertising) to tell you it is available.

In the case of a business-opportunity or investment scam, the fronter will dangle the prospect of phantom wealth right out of the gate. Recall our man Joe Vertega talking to the undercover investigator. Within the first five minutes, he is dangling phantom wealth:

> Now John, you'll be guaranteed to earn no less than $300 per phone. Per month. That is in writing. . . . So we expect you to recover your initial investment between the first seven to nine months. One hundred percent return.

Oil and gas fronters like Johnny Weber are even bolder with the use of phantom riches:

> We have had a lot of success drilling out here in the Gulf. For a minimum investment of $29,000, we've been able to show fellas returns in the neighborhood of $150,000.

31

The con artist will dangle the prospect of fast, easy money in the hope that the prospective victim will start to get excited. And if the phantom stimulus is strong enough, it might even activate the emotional centers of the brain and begin to create the coveted ether state.

Researchers analyzed hundreds of undercover fraud tapes and found that the phantom riches tactic was the single most common persuasion tactic employed by cons when pitching their victims.[2]

Qualifying the Victim

After the fronter has gotten the prospect interested by dangling easy phantom riches, the next step is to qualify the victim. A qualified victim has three characteristics: liquid assets to invest, a willingness to take risks, and the ability to be controlled.

First and foremost, the fronter has to find out if the prospect has the funds to go forward. Recall Joe Vertega in the very first call with the prospect:

> If I brought you in at an entry level with seven of the new general smart phones, you're looking at approximately a $15,000 overall investment. Are you capable of dealing with that?

If the prospect indicates an inability to make that kind of an investment, the call ends. The best fronters will not only qualify the money, but also find out where it is. Mike Harris said, "I was pretty bold about asking the prospect exactly where the money was, in a certificate of deposit (CD) or in a checking account. If they couldn't be specific about where the money was, it told me they might not actually have it."

If the scam is an unregistered investment like an oil and gas deal or a movie deal, many times the fronter will ask the prospect if he or she is an accredited investor, meaning someone who has a net worth of more than $1 million or has an annual income more than $200,000. Most fronters are more interested in verifying how much liquid cash the prospect has, but they go through the motions to ask about being an accredited investor because Securities and Exchange Commission (SEC) guidelines require it. Brokers can only sell unregistered securities to accredited investors.

In addition to finding the money, con artists are looking for prospects who are risk takers and who they can control. There are a variety of ways to determine willingness to take risks, but many cons will simply ask the victim if he or she has ever invested in things like business opportunities or oil and gas before. In terms of controllability, the con artist can get a sense of this by telling the prospect to do things. "I would ask the prospect to go turn down the television in the background to see if they would do it," said Ed Joseph. "I can also tell if they are controllable based on how many of my questions they answer."

Profiling

The key functions of a fronter are casting the net, dangling wealth, and qualifying the prospect in terms of money, risk taking, and controllability. Another key element in the fraud game is profiling: Learning personal details of the victim to later customize the pitch to match those details. This fraud tactic is typically done in the drive stage, but if the fronter is experienced and knows what he or she is doing, some profiling will be part of that first encounter with the victim.

Profiling is the process of identifying information that will motivate the victim to buy. It could be information about losing one's job, information about one's children—whatever can be picked up that can be used against the victim in the close. It is about asking probing, personal questions, listening to the answers, and writing them down for later use. Joseph says that master closers want to find out where the prospect's emotional vulnerability lies.

> In the first conversation, I am asking a lot of questions about the person's personal life. I want to know where they used to work, are they married, how long have they been married, what they have invested in before. I am looking for things they care about. What motivates them? Is it their grand kids? Is it improving their relationship with their wife? It's kind of like a jewelry thief casing the local jewelry store.

Edwards agrees completely: "Everyone has something in their life that they care so much about, they will do anything for it.

That first conversation is about asking questions, writing down the answers, and finding out what will move them into the ether. Because that's where it all happens."

Mike Harris said that he was trained to ask a lot of questions about the prospect so you could find out the hot buttons that would close the sale: "We were told that empathy was an important part of the sales process. If you can't get inside the head of the victim, you can't sell them. The rule of thumb is that to sell John Smith what John Smith buys, you must see John Smith through John Smith's eyes."

The most surprising thing about our con artists' descriptions of profiling is the sheer amount of time they spend focused on it. This underscores just how important it is to understand what motivates the victim before one can exploit him or her.

Stage Two—The Drive

Once the fronter has hooked the interest of the prospect, qualified the money, and found out as much personal information as possible about the person, then it's time to drive the sale. Edwards describes the drive as taking the person for a ride down the road you want them to go down, not necessarily the road that is best for them. There are essentially three elements to the drive: customizing the pitch, establishing credibility, and turning up the ether.

Customizing the Pitch

After the con artist has collected a profile of the prospect's emotional hot buttons, he or she is ready to customize the pitch. And while there is no question that cons will employ sophisticated combinations of persuasion tactics, the key to closing the sale is *matching persuasion tactics with emotional needs*. This takes us back to the literature on emotion and motivation. Identifying what motivates a person can be the key to manipulating them. Edwards explains:

> Let me give you an example. I find out through the profiling process that Joe Prospect just lost his job. I also find out that he is the principle bread winner in the family and his wife barely makes anything. He also tells me through the course of

conversation that his biggest fear is not being able to provide for his family. So the emotion to target is fear, which I throttle up on by saying something like:

Jim, tell me again how much your mortgage nut is each month? $3,100. Wow that must be a nice house. And yet you only have $50K left in the bank. Let me tell you something, if I were you, I would want to take some immediate action on that because providing a roof over your family should be your top concern right now.

Ed Joseph employed the same strategy. "I had a woman who I took for hundreds of thousands of dollars and very early on in my relationship with her, I realized that she was a deeply religious person. I spent hours praying with her, reading the Bible, establishing trust, and then I stole everything she had."

Harris focused on the ego. "If I was talking to a guy who seemed like he wanted to act real tough and macho, I would joke with him and say something like, 'We have a couple of secretaries in the office here who have bought full units for $100,000 each—how many are you going to buy?' And boy, they would chase after it then because their manhood was threatened."

Establishing Credibility

Fraud researchers analyzing investment fraud undercover audio-tapes found that one of the most common persuasion tactics was something called *source credibility*. It is the idea that to persuade a prospect to invest, the con artist must first convince the victim that he works for a credible operation.[3]

In addition to creating the external trappings of success as part of the illusion, the con establishes credibility by going over what seems like a lot of details about the deal. What the prospect does not know is that the con is very deliberate and selective about which details to focus on. As Mike Harris says, "When you are going over the packet, you never want to describe the entire thing. You only want to emphasize why the operation is credible and how much you will make. If they start getting into the rest of it, then it gets technical and that means they will want to bring in an outside expert—which you want to avoid at all costs."

Pioneers of Fraud: Charles Smyth

Charles "Doc" Smyth was a confidence man in the 1870s and 1880s

Charles Smyth was a New York-based confidence man in the 1870s and 1880s who was known as a "Sawdust Man." Sawdust men were notorious for mailing circulars all over the United States to farmers offering "green goods," a benign-sounding term for cheap counterfeit money. They would lure victims in with offers to buy $2,500 worth of counterfeit bills for as little as $200. Another variation on the scam was to mail out a circular with a fake news article that supposedly reported that a full set of dies and plates had been stolen from the U.S. Treasury, which was how they could offer authentic cash for so cheap.

When these con men met with the victim, they would show the cash, then switch bags at the last minute, leaving the victim holding a bag of sawdust.

The way they would identify potential victims was almost exactly the way it is done today. Consider this description of how sawdust men found their victims, written by New York City Police Commissioner Thomas Byrnes in 1886:

> The first move of sawdust men is to secure the list of names of people who were regular subscribers to lotteries and various gift-book concerns. People who go into these things will be pretty sure to bite on another scheme.[4]

Thus, even as early as 1886, con men were acutely aware that the best predictor of future behavior is past behavior, and so they purchased lists of individuals who had previously fallen for a similar type of scam.

The primary way that salespeople build credibility is to focus the prospect's attention on what are often glossy brochures showing expensive oil rigs and other equipment as well as focusing on past success. Listen to our con man Joe Vertega:

> This is the new generation Bell "Smart" phone actually. This phone has only been off the manufacturer line now for three years. During that period of time, I've placed literally thousands of these phones all across the United States and John, I've never had a single technical complaint on these phones.

In the case of business-opportunity fraud, a common way to establish false credibility is through the use of references. The reference's job is to help establish the credibility of the deal by posing as a current customer who just purchased the product and is making a lot of money. As you will see when we describe specific business-opportunity scams, it is not uncommon for the scam operation to employ multiple references or "singers" who will always sing the praises of the company, a task for which they are handsomely compensated.

These third-party endorsements are very effective because they reinforce that the investment is a good deal and allow the prospects to do some due diligence before investing, which makes them feel more comfortable.

Turn Up the Ether

Another goal for the con artist during the drive portion of the scam is to get the prospect excited by pointing out all the money that can be made. As we described in Chapter 2, if stimuli that appeal to the emotional centers of the brain are strong enough, those signals can actually bypass the rational centers and go directly to the emotional centers that can trigger a hijacking. Table 3.1 shows a list of the various persuasion tactics used to accomplish this.

"All throughout the drive, I try to emphasize the amount of money that can be made on the deal to get the juices flowing," said Edwards. His friend and former colleague Joe Vertega knew how to ratchet up the excitement during the drive.

> To show you where I want to take you, I want you to have no less than 50 telephones within 17 months maximum. Because your growth potential in your markets are—I mean—you could have 100 phones within two to three years very easily. Each

Table 3.1 Common Persuasion Tactics Used by Con Artists[5]

Tactic	Description
Phantom Riches	The con dangles something like a lucrative return on investment or huge prize to get the victim to invest or pay a processing fee.
Source Credibility	The con will make claims that link the operation to other credible organizations like big banks, federal agencies, or other trustworthy institutions.
Social Consensus	The con makes it appear that many people want in on the deal. The victim thinks, "If everyone is doing it, it must be good."
Scarcity	The con knows that making an object look scarce and rare increases its perceived value. Cons also use another form of scarcity known as the take away: If you don't want to invest, there are plenty of others who do.
Comparison	The con will compare the cost (or some other attribute) that the victims could be paying with what they are really paying. This can be done by comparing a higher price to a lower price.
Friendship	The con plays the role of someone who is friendly by saying "we have a lot in common," "I'm on your side," or "I have nothing to gain."

phone earns a minimum of $300 a month. Pay phones are a numbers game.

You can almost sense the ether building as these words leave Vertega's lips. He is turning up the gas as he approaches the close. Many of the business opportunity pitches build excitement by focusing (or driving) the prospect past the immediate sale to focus on future wealth. This not only increases the excitement, but also reinforces the long-term nature of the relationship, which helps build credibility.

Stage Three—The Close

After the con has customized the pitch, established credibility, and turned up the ether on the drive, it's time to begin the close. If the con has correctly executed the front and drive, the close is really fairly simple and straightforward. Different con artists have different styles of closing and even conceptualize it differently, but all of them seem to agree that there are three main parts: ask for the money, answer objections, and the take away.

Ask for the Money

This is an obvious part of the close, but according to our master closers, most people do not know when or how to ask for the money. One signal that the prospect is ready to be closed is that he or she starts talking about "my phones" or "my machine," which indicates that he or she is psychologically committed to buy. Sometimes, the con artist will encourage such behavior by describing the business by the prospect's name.

Vertega did that when he was on the phone with the undercover investigator. He was discussing growing the prospect's (John Swanson) business and he said, "Let's say Swanson Pay Phone simply reinvested earnings on the first seven phones. All of a sudden, you have 21 telephones." By inserting the prospect's name into the pitch, he is presumptively encouraging the prospect to identify as already having invested.

One reason this works is because of a phenomenon known as the *Endowment Effect*. This is a concept in psychology that once we own something, we perceive it as more valuable.[6] The simplest manifestation of this idea is as follows: Imagine you are walking down the street and you see a penny on the ground. Do you pick it up? Perhaps you do, perhaps you don't. Now imagine that you are walking down that same street and a penny falls out of your pocket. Do you pick it up? Probably. Why would you be more likely to pick up a penny that falls out of your pocket than one that is lying on the ground? Because the one that fell out of your pocket is *your* penny. Forget that in a pure rational economic sense, the penny on the ground is worth exactly as much as the penny that fell out of your pocket.

Just as there are clues about when to close, there are clues that the prospect is *not* ready to be closed. Edwards was a master at knowing when to close or not: "One way I know the prospect is not ready is when he is still challenging the deal. He will ask questions like, 'On page 32, it says that when the machine malfunctions, the company will do x, y, or z.' If they are still reading the paperwork, then I know they have not psychologically purchased yet."

Another indication that the prospect is still in the process of deciding whether to purchase is if he or she asks for more customers to interview. Trying to close at this point is a mistake many rookie closers make because it can lead to the prospect hanging up. Many boiler rooms would have veteran closers like Edwards supervise these transactions: "At the end of my career, I was not on the phone closing myself. But I was working in the rooms listening to other people close and coaching them on exactly this thing—when is the right and wrong time to ask for the sale."

Answering Objections

The art of answering objections is key to closing the sale. Mike Harris said he likes to think of a long hallway with open doors on either side. Each open door represents an objection that could allow the prospect to escape. His job is to get the prospect from one end of the hall to the other, closing each door just before the prospect gets to it.

Edwards says that the truly gifted closers will answer objections that are in the prospect's mind before they actually articulate that objection: "I always had a lot of empathy for the victim. I know it sounds strange—I don't mean sympathy—empathy. Like, I could read their mind or something and I always seemed to be able to sense when they were thinking of a reason not to invest. So I would jump in with an answer before they said it."

Edwards' contention is that if you wait until a prospect has actually articulated an objection, then it is harder to refute because saying it out loud gives the objection more power.

As part of a fraud prevention training video, Edwards reenacted the Federal Stimulus pitch where he was telling a prospect that for $279, he would guarantee that she would receive an $8,000 federal stimulus grant. Edwards was going to ask the victim for her checking account number so he could do a third-party demand draft. Anticipating that the prospect would object to this, Edwards went into an elaborate explanation of why doing an electronic transfer with the checking account number was absolutely the safest way to transact business because you can trace where the money came from and where it went. This is an example of anticipating and answering an objection before it is verbalized to avoid it gaining a head of steam.

The Take Away

The final element of the close is something known as the take away. The main approach in this phase of the close is to create urgency when the prospect is stalling on making a decision. So when the prospect says he wants to think about it or he wants to ask his lawyer or his wife, the con artist will come in with some kind of statement about how many other people are interested in this particular item or how few are left.

One reason this approach has the effect of getting people to act is that it appeals to that part of the emotional brain that instinctively wants to avoid loss. For thousands of years, we humans have been conditioned to panic when there is a threat of running out of food or water. It is part of our evolutionary past. The con artist taps into this emotional survival impulse by threatening to take away the investment.

Federal Stimulus Scam—The Front

Jim: Good afternoon Pat. My name is Jim and I represent a company by the name of National Grants. Somewhere down the line, you expressed an interest in being eligible for federal stimulus grant money. We're finally getting back to you with a phone call. I have some great news Pat. You've been deemed eligible for a minimum of $8,000 to a maximum of $25,000 federal grant. As I said, it's part of the $500 billion stimulus package that was passed earlier this year by Congress. And it's basically put in place to get the economy moving again.

Here at National Grants, we believe the fat cats on Wall Street have gotten their piece of the pie and now it's time for people on Main Street to get theirs. Am I right? Let me ask you one question

Pat—everybody has something in mind they would spend between $8,000 and $25,000 on—what do you have in mind?

Pat: Probably some home repairs.

Jim: Yeah, I gotta tell ya—I do this day in and day out and we can handle and process about fifty applications a day. And we are overwhelmed with the response. I would say that about 97 percent of the people we speak to on a daily basis move forward with this. Because it's very safe—it's risk free and it's guaranteed. And I would say probably 40 to 50 percent of the people that I speak to personally—and I have four other people who make these calls similar to the calls that I make—are doing home improvements. And they are not even home improvements— they're necessary repairs that need to be done. They're oil burners, roofs, replacing electrical panel boxes. I don't know how people would get this stuff done if they didn't have access to this stimulus money.

Federal Stimulus Scam—The Drive

Jim: Now our job is to cut through the red tape and speed up and facilitate the process of getting that money to you. We have been in business for eight years and our focus back when we first started was to help people like yourself get government grants back when grants were hard to get. As a result of this stimulus package, the goal is to spread the wealth, so getting a grant has become easy. I mean, not everyone out there knows this, but basically if you have a Social Security number, are over the age of 18, and have a pulse, you're eligible for stimulus money. But unless somebody like me calls you on the phone and tells you that, you don't know it. And without our help, it could take up to 18 months The most important thing for you to understand is that this is not a loan. This is not money that you have to pay back—this is a grant. We do not take a percentage of that grant or anything like that—it's a one-time fee and I'll get into that with you and explain to you how that works. Based on your answers to the application that we're going to send out to you and which you will send back to my legal department, that's going to tell us exactly how much you're eligible for.

Federal Stimulus Scam—The Close

Jim: Now as I said, it is a one-time fee of $279 and basically what we do is an electronic transaction and the reason for this is for your safety and protection as well as ours. I'm sure you're aware that an electronic transaction is the safest way to do anything because what it does is it leaves an electronic fingerprint. So we know where it came from and you know where you sent it. And when you have an electronic transaction, you have the recourse to reverse it. So rather than ask for a cashier's check or a personal check or anything like that, we do this electronically. And again, it's a one-time fee of $279.

Now I want you to understand something. We have a guarantee in place. And the guarantee simply states that if for any reason you do not receive your money within eight months, we will return the $279 in full, no questions asked.

So for this one-time fee of $279, you are guaranteed a minimum of $8,000 up to $25,000 based on some of the particulars in the application that we are going to send out to you. That's going to be sent back to the legal department and from there you can go online with the number that's on the application and you can check the status and it will show you where it's at, who has it now, how close it is to approval, and how close you are to actually receiving a check.

Pat: I'm just hesitating slightly because you know one is always concerned about like giving out a checking account number on the phone—do you have anything in writing that I can receive before giving you my checking account number?

Jim: Well, I tell you what, you already have my phone number, you could go to our web site. The only thing that worries me is simply this. We can only process 50 applications a day because there is a lot of paperwork that needs to be done and you know the stars have to align in a certain way to get this done for everybody. And I don't want you to get lost in the shuffle right now. Right now you are on the phone with me and we have the opportunity to move forward.

The reason why we set this up as a company to go forward with electronic transactions is to ease that feeling that you have right now. If you're uncomfortable with giving me your checking account information, that's why we give you the option to put it on a major credit card. I'm sure you are aware of how protected you are with a major credit card. All you have to do is call the credit card company and say "Hey, I want to reverse this charge."

Pat: You're right—that might be a preferable way to do this. Let me give you my Visa card.

Stage Four—The Load

The load is the process of re-victimizing the prospect soon after he or she has been taken. While it may seem counter-intuitive that a victim would agree to a second investment, con artists say it is in some ways easier than the first sale. The basic structure of the load is surprise, creating a new development, and urgency.

Surprise

Persuasion experts have known for years that if you can see a persuasive attempt coming from a distance, you are better able to defend against it.[7] Most investors do not expect to be re-contacted a week after making a large investment. Thus, when the con artist calls back to let the victim know about a new opportunity, the investor is caught off guard. While he or she may be surprised, the victim is willing to listen because it is too soon after the first sale for the investment to have failed.

A New Development

The con artist will call the victim back and act like something big and unexpected has just occurred. To add to the drama of the moment, the con artist will close the door to the office and tell the victim that the new development is "so hot and so potentially lucrative that [I] don't want others around the office to know about it." Then the scenario is described:

- A customer bought eight units, but the warehouse just burned down, so the company needs to sell the phones to someone else for half price.
- A customer bought half a dozen units, but then a relative in Europe passed away unexpectedly, so he has been out of the country for six weeks and needs to dump the product for a fraction of the regular cost.
- An investor was going to buy a full unit in the oil deal, but couldn't free up the cash at the last minute, so there is an extra unit available.

This approach of creating a new development that leads to opportunity serves to reignite the ether that was created when the victim was closed in the first place. It also catches him or her off guard, which makes it difficult to come up with a refusal script and resist. In addition, the idea that a second investment would be taking advantage of an unexpected but profitable situation taps into a strongly held belief among many investors that changing market conditions are what create opportunity. Edwards says he would reinforce this by telling the prospect that many fortunes have been made by people who can respond quickly to changing market conditions.

Urgency

One of the ways that con men reinforce urgency is to use multiple voices in the load. Edwards perfected the idea of using locators to double-team victims during the load. A locator in the business-opportunity game is an ally of the con artist, who plays the role of the person who will locate attractive spots to place the vending machine,

DVD dispenser, or Internet kiosk the prospect is buying. Depending on how the scam is run, the locator can be brought in during the close or, as is more often the case, during the load, to be a third voice who reinforces the urgent nature of the current situation.

Table 3.2   The Stages of Fraud

Stage	Tactic
The Front	**Cast the Net**—Reach many people through phone calling, TV/radio, or print advertising. **Dangle Phantom Riches**—Make appealing claims about one's investment in a year or less. **Qualify the Victim**—Make sure the client is liquid enough to have the money to invest. **Profile the Victim**—Gather personal information about the victim.
The Drive	**Customize the Pitch**—Match the pitch to previously identified personal information/emotional needs. **Build Credibility**—Paint a picture of a wildly successful business and provide (fake) references. **Turn up the Ether**—Repeat claims about income potential to heighten emotions.
The Close	**Ask for the Money**—Ask for the sale at the right time. Answer Objections—Anticipate and isolate objections and answer them quickly. **Take Away**—Build urgency by claiming to have only so much time or product left.
The Load	**Surprise**—Catch the victim off guard by calling back within a week or two. **New Development**—Describe a surprising development that taps into the entrepreneurial spirit. **Urgency**—Create urgency by emphasizing the time-limited nature of the opportunity.

Conclusion

Con artists employ a variety of tactics to defraud their victims. See Table 3.2 for an outline of the stages of fraud. By understanding the stages that the con artists puts victims through, you can begin to understand how the process works and therefore be able to defend against it. Now it's time to see these tactics and stages in action.

PART II

CON ARTISTS IN ACTION

4

Exploiting Ego

The Oil-and-Gas Scam

The kind of people I deal with can take $150,000 in cash, burn it in the fireplace, and never give it another thought. You're playing with the big boys now. Can you handle that?
—Mike Harris, former oil-and-gas closer

Oilfield Investments (not its real name) was a fraudulent oil-and-gas boiler room operation that was shut down by the U.S. Securities and Exchange Commission (SEC) in 2007. Before it was sued for multiple violations of federal securities laws, Oilfield's operators took in more than $14 million dollars from investors and squandered all of the money on nightclubs, expensive cars, drugs, and alcohol, leaving investors with virtually nothing.

While stories about these types of scams are all too common these days, what is unique about this story is that it is told from the perspective of two individuals who have intimate knowledge about the Oilfield Investments scam:

Steve Johnson, a 57-year-old stockbroker who lost $40,000 of his retirement funds by investing in the Oilfield scam;

Johnny Weber, the 38-year-old former owner/operator of Oilfield, who pleaded guilty to investment fraud in December 2009. In 2010, Weber provided an extensive interview that revealed many of the tricks he taught his salesmen. The same day we interviewed Weber, he was ordered to serve a 10-year sentence in federal prison.

Their stories offer an unprecedented inside look at how fraudulent oil and gas companies work and the challenges law enforcement faces in stopping this crime. While the facts described are true, the names of the individuals and companies have been changed, and any similarity between pseudonyms used and real companies is coincidental. As you will see, oil and gas scams like Oilfield follow the four stages of fraud outlined in the previous chapter.

The Front

Fraudulent oil and gas operations cast the net to find victims in a variety of ways, but most use cold calling as their primary strategy. In this sense, Oilfield Investments was typical. Oilfield had 50 to 60 fronters working in three separate boiler rooms making between 150 and 200 calls per day each. They called people whose names appeared on lead lists they had purchased from lead brokers. Johnny Weber describes how the fronter pitch went in his operation:

> Johnny: Hi, is Steve there please? Steve this is John over at Oilfield Investments, you remember me? The reason for my call is I know you had requested some information on investments to enrich your portfolio. Somewhere along the lines, you were looking for anywhere from 5-to-1 to 10-to-1 on your money, is that correct? Great. Great news. I have a couple of projects that I wanted to run by you because I believe they would be a perfect fit for your portfolio.

The first thing right out of the gate with oil and gas pitches is dangling phantom wealth to draw in investors. Then he goes on to explain the tax benefits:

> Johnny: Now are you familiar with the tax advantages that go along with oil and gas as well? With oil and gas investments, you can write off 100 percent of your investments. 80 to 85 percent you can write off the first year, and 15 to 20 percent

is amortized over the next 5 to 10, years depending on how aggressive you are. So that right there, you could possibly write off 100 percent of the investment.

The fronter starts by dangling a 5-to-1 or 10-to-1 return, but then adds the additional feature that the whole investment is tax deductible, which is an important factor for many investors. Most of the calls made out of these boiler rooms result in hang ups or "No Thank You" or just "No!" But in 10 to 15 percent of the cases, the person on the other end of the line will listen and maybe even begin to answer questions.

In the first phone call, the fronter will try to quickly establish that the investor has enough net worth to be an accredited investor and enough liquid assets to immediately write a large check. As Johnny Weber said, "The most important things they are trying to get out of you in the first call or two is what have you invested in and what are you liquid for: What could you write me a check for today?"

Johnny says that many times, it will take two or three calls to get this information out of an investor. If there is initial resistance, the fronter will drop the oil and gas pitch and switch to building the relationship. He taught his salespeople a system known as FORM: Family, Occupation, Recreation, Motivation. The fronter will ask the investor questions in each of these areas. This accomplishes two things. First, it shows that the salesperson is interested on a personal level, which helps build the relationship, and second, it provides the salesperson with personal profiling information.

"People love to talk about themselves," Johnny explains, "so the salesman will ask key questions about those four points and it opens them up and lowers their guard. What are they motivated by? What recreation do they do? Are they golfers? What is the victim's hot button? Is it children? Is it money? Is it retirement? Do they want to be on a yacht when they are 50, do they want to be aggressive with their investments so they can retire early?"

As we discussed in Chapter 2, many con artists have told us they are looking for the victim's emotional hot buttons to put them under the ether. Steve Johnson said that the first several calls he received from Oilfield involved asking him questions about his past investing history: "They asked me about my situation and I told them I needed to make a higher return on my portfolio so I could retire on time. I felt like I needed to be honest with them so they could match me with the right investment. At least that is how I operate when I'm dealing with my clients."

But the questions didn't end with the types of investments he had made. "The salesmen asked me all about my personal life and he told me all about his personal life," he said. "I knew all about his kids, his wife, what problems they had. Over time we became friends." Steve told the Oilfield salesmen that even though he was a financial planner himself, he didn't feel prepared for retirement. He had just put his daughter through eight years of college and was about to pay for her expensive wedding. And at age 58, he began to realize that if he was ever going to be able to retire, he would have to start taking more risks to make more on his investments.

In retrospect, Steve realizes that he gave the Oilfield salesman a lot of ammunition to use to sell him. "The thing is that sharing your personal situation with a broker—a legitimate broker—is a normal part of the process. I know a lot of personal information about all of my clients. The difference is, I use it to offer advice that is in their best interest. These guys were asking it so they could more easily exploit my situation. And it worked."

The Drive

The drive is done differently depending on the personality of the investor. Johnny taught his salesmen that a key part of the drive was not only to understand the investor's basic motivations, but also to specifically place them into one of four discrete personality types.

"I taught my guys that every one of the 6.3 billion people in this world are in one of the four personality types: accepting, promoter, analytical, and driver."

Accepting—"The accepting personality is someone who is easy-going and spontaneous. As an animal, they would be a lamb. They are tree huggers—they want to make everyone else comfortable. Think about your gramma."

Promoter—"The promoter is assertive and spontaneous. As an animal, the promoter is a tiger. They like to dress nice, they are the ones that puff out their chest, and they are always talking about themselves. They are very outgoing, a people-person type. Promoters are usually your salesmen—they are all about persona."

Drivers—"Drivers are assertive and self controlled. They are the bulls. They are usually your CEOs. They are the visionaries—they make things happen. They are very headstrong—you don't want to compete with a driver. They will run right over you. And with drivers, a lot of times you will hear them say things like 'bottom line—don't waste my time.'"

Analytics—"These are your engineers, the accountants. They are all about the numbers. Don't try to paint a pretty picture for them, don't try to throw compliments to them—it's hey, the numbers need to make sense and I need to see the numbers in black and white."

Johnny provides these four basic personality types in his training so that the salespeople can customize their pitches to match the personality types. He provides an example: "We would do role plays. Let's say you are on the phone and you are hearing, 'Hey I don't have a lot of time to talk—what do you want?' Okay what personality type is that? A driver personality type. I would show the guys how to handle a driver personality."

> Johnny: Mr. Jones, I totally understand this call was not set in your appointment book—real quick, um. My name is Johnny Weber, Oilfield Investments. They said that you sent out some information, wanted to do some investing with your portfolio. I have a project that will fit perfectly—bottom line, 10 to 1 on your money. If I can show you that, would you be interested?
>
> Investor: Yeah, I just don't have time.
>
> Johnny: Totally understand, I'm not trying to waste your time right now. What would be a good time that I could call you back to go over the details and see if this would be a good fit for your portfolio?
>
> Investor: Well I don't know.

Johnny: Totally understand—are mornings or afternoons better for you.

Investor: Afternoons.

Johnny: Okay I have a 1:30 or a 3:00 open on my appointment book—which would work better?

Investor: 1:30.

Johnny: Okay, do you have a pen in front of you?

Johnny is modeling for his salespeople in training how you modify your approach to fit into one of the four personality types. With a driver personality, you need to be all business and not mess around and waste time. With a promoter personality, it's a different approach. "With a promoter personality, I would go into painting the picture of excitement."

Johnny: Hey man did you hear about the new 'vette that just came out? Can you believe that it has this much horsepower on it? Have you thought about getting one of those, or what's your favorite car?

Investor: Oh I like the Lamborghini Gallardo.

Johnny: Really well let me ask you a question, have you got one yet?

Investor: No man but I've been saving for it.

Johnny: How much does it cost—sticker price?

Investor: $275,000.

Johnny: Really so let me ask you this. If on a couple of my oil and gas projects, if I could take care of that for you, you wouldn't be mad? I'd probably get a Christmas card, huh?

Investor: Oh yea, ha, ha, ha.

This is another example of customizing the pitch to meet the emotional needs of the victim. A promoter personality likes fast cars and excitement. Other personality types do not.

"The analytical personality is completely different from the promoter. He's not really about pretty rainbows and talking about what he and the wife did on the last vacation. He likes doing the numbers himself on his portfolio, he likes sitting there and doing day trading on his time off. That's his hot button. So the next time you talk to him, you can say, 'Hey did you hear about Dow Corp., or did you hear about what was going on with Lockheed Martin the other day with their stock portfolio?' 'No, I didn't—tell me about it.' Boom. Now you have an open end—now you are hitting a hot button on him."

It is not at all clear whether the social-science community would agree with Johnny that all of humanity can be neatly divided into four discrete personality types as he describes. There is well-established literature in psychology known as *The Big Five* personality traits that is similar to Johnny's model, although the five traits are described differently and are infinitely more grounded in research.[1] What his system does illustrate is the extent to which con artists work at profiling their victims and then customizing the pitch to match that profile. It is also another reminder of how gifted con artists must be at empathizing and reading their victims' personalities in order to swindle them.

If you are dealing with a registered broker who is selling a registered product, the chances are good that sharing some personal information with them to help legitimately customize your portfolio to meet your needs is safe. If you are dealing with an unregistered oil and gas operation out of Texas, sharing personal information about yourself can be dangerous. As Ed Joseph said, a con man asking personal questions is like the burglar casing a jewelry store before robbing it. If you can find out where all the expensive jewelry is located, where the security cameras are hidden, and how many people are working and when, then you know the easiest way to get in and out without getting caught.

Once the fronter had qualified Steve and found out about his personal situation, it was time to send him a prospectus to go over and set up an appointment for three to five days later. Here is how Johnny would set up the close:

Johnny: Steve, you are going to have the packet in front of you, we're going to go over it from start to finish and I am going to need to clear your schedule for about 25 to 30 minutes. And in the meantime, I want you to look over the packet, do your final due diligence, and let's go over everything in black and white because at the end of that, I'm going to ask you to write a check for the $50,000 that you said you are liquid for.

Johnny would then commit the investor to a "close" call three to five days later and mail out the packet. What he wouldn't tell the investor is that in a couple of days, he was going to call him with the mark call. A mark call is an unscheduled call the con artist makes to the investor prior to the close call that verifies that he got the packet, reminds him to read it, and continues to build the relationship.

Johnny: Hey Steve, how's it going—just wanted to check on how the kids are doing. Okay. Well I know that we had scheduled to talk on Tuesday at 7 PM—I got you in my calendar—you got me? Great Okay. A couple of things. One—did you check out the price of oil today—$70? Great. I'm going to talk about that on the call Tuesday. I know that I am just a speck on the wall until I start making you money, so I just wanted to make sure I was in your calendar. I got you in mind. I'll talk to you then.

The Close

Steve Johnson was very impressed by the package he received from Oilfield. "The company sent me all these nice, glossy four-color brochures that tend to make you think that they're legit because producing all those documents in four-color is a very expensive venture. Someone spent some money. And I later learned they spent $75,000 dollars producing those particular documents. But, you know, if you're scamming people out of money, you can afford $75,000."

A key part of the close according to Johnny is focusing the investor's attention only on those portions of the printed material that will lead to the sale:

The only thing you want to show the investor is the prospectus. If it's a good prospectus, it's telling a story from start to finish.

What the credibility of the company is, what your intent is, the pretty pictures showing the graphics, the income potential, and then it goes to the close on it. I tell my guys, "Buyers are not readers and readers are not buyers." So if they are asking you lots of questions about the paperwork, they're probably not buyers anyway.

Steve says that was his experience as well. "They focused my attention primarily on the money I could make and the success they had had with previous drilling. I was told that for my initial $20,000 investment, my total return would be about $100,000 over five years. My expectation was a five-to-one return."

But why didn't Steve (and many others) ask more questions and more carefully read the paperwork? Johnny has an answer:

They don't have enough information to take control of the conversation. You have them open-minded now. They are following more than they are trying to lead you. They want to grasp everything: How this can affect their pocketbook, how it could affect their kids college, how it could make their life easier so they are not crossing the Ts and dotting the Is, they are focusing more on the end result. How do I get to make money? How do I get mailbox money coming in every month?

After spending approximately 30 minutes selectively pointing out parts of the investment package he could use to persuade Steve to invest, the Oilfield salesman led him to the final document where Steve was asked to fill out a suitability questionnaire that had him confirm his net worth and that he had received and read all pertinent documents. Among those documents was something called the Confidential Information Memorandum, a 57-page, single-spaced tome that contained all kinds of disclosures and disclaimers about the transaction.

In his 30-minute presentation with Steve, the Oilfield salesman never once mentioned this document, much less pointed out the numerous items within it. Yet Steve was required to sign a form stating that he had read and understood everything in that document.

Among the disclosures in that document that the Oilfield salesman did not choose to focus on (bold emphasis added):

- Investment in the interests involves a **high degree of risk**, potential **conflicts of interest**, and substantial compensation to the managing venturer (Oilfield)
- The managing venturer (Oilfield) will receive a one-time management fee in the amount of **$1,467,500**
- The compensation to the managing venturer (Oilfield), although believed by the managing venturer to be comparable to compensation charged by managers in other similar ventures, **has not been the subject of arm's-length negotiations**
- The managing venturer (Oilfield) is entitled to **receive compensation** and reimbursement authorized by the joint venture agreement **regardless of whether the joint venture operates at a profit or a loss**

The $1.467 million fee for the managing partner written into these agreements was particularly outrageous for two reasons. First, it represented a full 25 percent of the total amount they proposed to raise for the project. Secondly, the Oilfield salesman told Steve directly that the costs of this operation would be lower than most because the driller had a financial interest in keeping costs down.

Johnny says there are three main tactics used in closing an oil-and-gas deal that he taught his boiler room people:

- Indifference (It doesn't matter to me if you do this—I get paid either way.)
- The Jones effect (You're an accountant? I have at least 10 accountants who have bought into this.)
- Take away (We only have three units left and they are going quickly so if you don't act quickly, you will lose out.)

Of these three, the take away was used the most. "No matter how many units an oil and gas company has, they only have two to five units to sell," says Johnny. Steve experienced this several times in his dealings with Oilfield.

"The Oilfield salesmen were always referring to the fact that there was a shortage of units, and that they were trying to get some more," said Steve. "They told me the units are going very quickly, and if you don't get 'em now, they won't be available. But, somehow, those additional units always turned up. The rep would call and say, 'You know, I had a guy that couldn't take this unit. And so I'm splitting it up among several investors and holding a part of it for you.' I later learned that the project was oversold, meaning that they sold more units than they actually had."

Johnny said every salesman in any profession is trained to answer objections like:

1. I need to think about it.
2. I need to run this by my attorney.
3. I don't do anything without consulting with my broker.
4. I have to run this by my wife.
5. I don't know who you or your company are.
6. I don't have any money right now.
7. I'm not doing any new investing this year.
8. I'm cash poor right now.

But the objection one would think was the most difficult to overcome turns out to be the easiest: "I lost money in a previous oil-and-gas scam." Johnny says selling previous oil-and-gas victims is easy because (a) they have already shown they take risks, and (b) they want to make it back, just like a gambler.

> Johnny: It's ridiculous. It's like an investing bug. He's got to have it. He's going to put up a strong fight, but once you answer all those questions and you build that relationship, he's going to go again and think, okay this time I'm going to hit 21—I'm going to hit Blackjack.

Johnny says the key to selling such a person is to let him vent about the previous transaction: "A lot of times you just have to sit there and let them unload on you about their last deal. He'll tell you what they did wrong, how they never returned his phone calls, never let him know exactly what was going on in the field, how he always had to call them—well, that's bullets for your gun right there. You isolate what they did wrong, then you tell the investor how you would do it differently."

> Johnny: So what I'm hearing you tell me, Mr. Investor, is if I get anything new in the field and a pump goes out, I need to let you know about it. It's just a five-minute call, whether it's good, bad, or indifferent, as long as I am calling and telling you first hand, you're okay with that?
>
> Investor: Yes, that's what I am talking about.
>
> Johnny: Okay, that's not going to be a problem here. Now, moving on—what was your next problem with that company?

Jimmy Edwards had an acronym for this closing technique. He referred to as LIRRC: listen, isolate, restate, rebut, and close. Although Johnny Weber and Jimmy Edwards have never met, they sure seem to share a common understanding of what it takes to steal from investors.

The Load

After convincing Steve to make the initial $20,000 investment, the Oilfield salesman called Steve back a month later and used fake oil-production reports and fake references to close him on the second $20,000 investment he would make in the company. As Steve recalls:

> The sales rep gave me oil-production documents that later proved to be false and he also gave me the name of another investor like myself who had put money into the project. This guy told me he had actually physically gone to the well site and seen all 15 wells. So he verified that for me. I kept calling him back and saying, "I think there are some problems," and he kept saying, "No, I've seen those wells. They're there." So his having seen the site is what convinced me to put in the second $20,000.

Steve said even though he invested a second $20,000, he was pressured to invest a lot more. He said the Oilfield salesmen called him once a week for months after he made the first investment, trying to reload him.

As our con experts have said, you want to reload the victim before the emotional ether has worn off. Once the victim comes to his senses and realizes the whole thing is a scam, it's over.

Conclusion

The story of Oilfield Investments clearly demonstrates how the four stages of fraud work in the real world. This company was shut down by the SEC in November 2007 and agreed to permanently discontinue its business in March 2008. At that time, a receiver was appointed to try to identify assets that could be distributed to the several hundred investors who had invested more than $14 million in the scheme. At its peak, Oilfield Investments had dozens of salespeople operating out of three different offices and they were taking in as much as $1 million per month from investors all over the country. In the end, less than $500,000 in assets were recovered and individual investors stand to get back less than 5 percent of their investments.

As he heads to federal prison, Johnny Weber continues to insist that his operation could have made money for investors if the government hadn't shut him down, but he also admits that there are a lot of fraudulent oil-and-gas rooms out there:

> Unfortunately, there are a lot of rooms that sell fraudulent interests in oil wells. When it comes to telemarketing, I would say at best, 3 to 5 percent of the people who might call you with an oil-and-gas investment are legitimate and 95 to 98 percent are scams.

Steve Johnson said his dealings with Oilfield have been devastating. "The money I invested with Oilfield was not money I could afford to lose. I was so sucked into this thing that I took out a second mortgage on my home to make that second $20,000 investment. Now I'm afraid I will never be able to retire."

Tips for Avoiding Oil and Gas

- Never make a buying decision when you are in a heightened emotional state (under the ether).

- Before investing in an oil-and-gas deal, find answers to the following questions:
    - Is the firm incorporated?
    - Are the brokers registered with the state securities regulator or with the Financial Industry Regulatory Authority (FINRA)?
    - Is the investment registered with the state securities regulator or with the SEC?
    - Is the SEC or FINRA investigating them?
    - If they claim to be exempt, have they filed a Regulation D form?

If either the broker or the investment is not registered, consider saying no to the investment.

To find out more about how you can avoid investment fraud, log onto the FINRA Foundation's web site at: www.saveandinvest .org/ProtectYourMoney/.

CHAPTER

Exploiting Faith

The Religious Ponzi Scam

We don't want anyone in the program that is a continual doubter.
Amen? If I catch you doubting, guess what happens? You come out.
Even if you are in for six million, seven million, doesn't make any
difference, you are coming out. Now why would we do that? Lack
of faith. The Lord said he couldn't do anything in his home town
because of lack of faith.
　　　—George Pride, co-founder of Globadine Ministries

From 1989 until 1999, Globadine Ministries (not its real name) built a congregation of more than 18,000 people throughout the United States based on its so-called *Faith Promise Plan.* The *promise* was that any money donated to the church in this program would be doubled in 17 months. The basis for this claim was:

1. The church had connections all over the world that allowed it to access secret and highly profitable gold and silver mining.
2. The foundation of the program was right there in the Bible. Luke 6:38 says give and you shall receive. "The Bible doesn't say give and you *might* receive" says Globadine co-founder Ron Mann. "It says give and you *shall* receive."

Over a 10-year period, members/victims of the Globadine Ministries church invested more than $450 million dollars in the Faith Promise Plan program. In August 1999, federal marshals and several dozen SWAT-team members driving armored tanks raided the Globadine Ministries offices in Florida and arrested the principals of the firm. The co-founders of the operation, George Pride and Ron Mann, along with several others, were charged with and convicted of running a massive Ponzi scheme, where they were collecting investment money from one investor to pay off other investors. Pride and Mann were sentenced to long prison terms. As the initial lawsuit charged:

> Globadine Ministries' money-doubling program is, has been, and continues to be, in fact, a con game and securities fraud. The scheme targets and preys primarily upon fundamentalist Christians and Christian sects but is not necessarily limited to them.

The description of the scheme continued:

> Globadine and its officers solicited investments with the promise that the funds invested would be doubled as the ultimate result of the blessings of God and as the product of Globadine Ministries' personnel who are able to profitably discern the will of the Supreme Being to make the funds grow through their reinvestment activities.

The suit alleges that no such profits were in fact discerned or achieved. How could this happen? How could so many members of various faith communities around the country fall for what was, to any rational-minded outsider, an obvious Ponzi scheme? Double your money in 17 months—guaranteed? Sounds crazy right? It was crazy unless all of your friends and fellow parishioners had been doing it and, at least at first, were getting back the promised return. It was crazy if you hadn't attended one of Globadine's church services and gotten caught up in the spiritual ether of believing that the money you gave was being spent to do the Lord's work.

And it was crazy unless you were someone who believed conspiracy theories about how the government was out to get all religious people and take their money.

These were just some of the powerful tactics employed in what was one of the scariest and most cruel scams we have ever seen— one that preyed on individual's faith in God, faith in other people, and fear of a corrupt society and government.

Ironically, Globadine Ministries was insistent on videotaping virtually every presentation they ever gave about the program, which was tremendously helpful to prosecutors. Transcripts of those tapes were filed in court as part of the prosecution's case against Globadine that led to the principals' convictions.[1] What follows are excerpts from one of these tapes that documents precisely how these con artists induced their victims to gift millions of dollars over to the "church"— money that was, for many, their life savings.

The Front

Globadine Ministries first cast the net to attract victims by infiltrating church congregations. It began with preachers like Ron Mann integrating the Promise Plan Program into guest sermons and then, after several dozen parishioners invested and started getting the promised returns, word started to spread like wildfire. What better way to run a Ponzi scheme than to start in a church where there is a high degree of trust, where large groups of people spend a lot of time together and tend to follow each other into business transactions. Once the program began to grow, the operation moved to giving workshops in hotels all across the south and eventually all across the United States.

The first impression one gets when watching video of the Globadine Ministries pitch is that it is nothing more than a lively Pentecostal church service. Long before co-founders George Pride or Ron Mann ever take the stage to describe the program, evangelical singers filled with the spirit of God go in front of the crowd and belt out rousing renditions of spiritual songs with full audience participation. After 45 to 50 minutes of singing, the whole room is worked up into a spiritual frenzy and every word uttered is punctuated with a vibrant "hallelujah" or "Amen, Brother." By the time Ron Mann is introduced, the crowd is clearly under the ether.

The pitch you are about to read was delivered in 1999 in Mobile, Alabama, just before the operation was closed down. Mann begins by discussing the role Globadine Ministries is playing doing the Lord's work:

> Mann: Our ministry has been going about 2,000 years now. Our part of the ministry has been about 37 years. This phase of the ministry—the gifting program—is going on 10 years. So how many know that we've not just started yesterday. You've heard that we've given out—we're not in the hundreds of millions—now we're up into the billion mark. How many are thankful for that—that a church can have a billion dollars? Amen? Well, you know that the Vatican has had that for a long time. But it's a miracle that a Pentecostal church has got that now—Amen—woooo—Hallelujah. It's time, as brother George said, that we take money from the heathen and we given it to the righteous. And how many is glad to get it? Amen.

Right from the start, Mann incorporates biblical concepts into his pitch and even compares Globadine Ministries to the Catholic church in terms of its financial success. But before he pitches the Faith Promise Plan, he does a little more preaching/pitching about two services they had conducted where they had laying on of hands and miracle healing:

> Mann: I want you to put your eyes on these tapes right over here. We have a series of tapes here that if you want to see the miracle meeting we had in Lebanon, we have on these two tapes a service where we had about 1,500 people in this service and it has a prayer line on it and everything. You see people getting healed and you hear them testifying and some of them got healed even before they got up to us. They said, "While we were in line, something warm went through my body and I don't have that pain no more." How

many know that's just like Jesus. How many know it's not man that's doing the work—it's God doing the work. And this set of tapes here—if you give a donation of $30, you can have those two.

This is a good example of how the front in this scam is a convoluted mixture of preaching and pitching, with constant references to Jesus and God and the work of the Lord, interspersed with requests for money. He continues:

Mann: What we do is we take the money you give and we ship it overseas and do what we call world trades with world banks. And we make 30 to 40 percent on our money each trade.

Here we have the first claim of phantom wealth. But in addition to making world trades, Globadine also apparently had a thriving gold and silver mining exploration business—or so they claimed.

Mann: In Liberia, the Prime Minister has opened the doors to Globadine Ministries and has given us an embassy suite there in that country, with 10 bedrooms, eight bathrooms, and two kitchens. How many can thank God for that embassy? They don't want some mineral deposit place coming in, they want a church coming in and they invited Globadine Ministries in and we're sending over hundreds and thousands of shovels, and now people in Africa can dig gold and diamonds and give it to Globadine and they can have money to buy their own food and medicine with and how many of you are glad you are part of this great movement of God? Amen.

Why do you think God let Globadine Ministries have its own gold coins and silver coins? Why do you think that God said in the depths of his earth is his riches? Is that scripture? Did you know that this last month or two we are living that scripture? That people in Africa are digging in their back yards and the riverbeds and they are getting diamonds out of their back yards worth $38,000? How many thankful for that?

The Drive

Once he describes some of the great wealth Globadine has and what it is doing with it to serve the Lord, Mann describes the Faith Promise Plan:

> Mann: Okay, how many know that the lowest you can come into the program is $250? Everybody say $250. The highest you can come into the program is $100 million in the morning and $100 million in the evening. How many want to start there at the highest part? Somewhere between $250 and $200 million, you will fit into that category. Regardless of what you donate to the church, we will put it into increments of $250, $500, 1, 2, 3, 4, $5,000—you see it on your donation form there on the right. If you put in a $250 increment only, or a $500 increment only, or a $1,000 increment only, you will not receive anything for six months. Everybody say six months—six.
>
> On the seventh month—everybody say the seventh month—on the seventh month—if you gave $250, you will receive $50 dollars a month for 10 months which would give you back how much? $500. That's double what? $250. If you came in at a $500 increment, on the seventh month, you would receive $100 a month for 10 months, which is $1,000 and is double your $500. If you put in $1,000 increment only, on the seventh month, you would receive $200 a month for 10 months, which would give you how much? $2,000 back for the $1,000 you put into the program in 16 months.

What Mann is describing is a mathematical formula that allows Globadine to take money from one parishioner, wait six months before starting to pay them back and then use that float to pay other people—a classic Ponzi scheme, only on an enormous scale. But what may seem obvious to an outsider is lost on those trapped under the ether—the faithful.

Nora Anderson was one of those faithful who was trapped in the religious ether. In the mid-1990s, Nora and her husband, Bob, were enjoying a hectic but fulfilling life raising seven children in a suburb of Portland, Oregon, when tragedy struck. A mentally disturbed neighbor came into their home, began arguing with Bob, and shot him at point blank range, killing him instantly. At that moment, Nora's entire world changed. She was faced with having to go back to work, find daycare for her seven children, and somehow make enough money to raise them all.

Nora also began to attend church more regularly, and in 1998 a friend at church told her about this amazing new investment program where thousands of people were putting in money and having it doubled in a short period of time. The friend showed Nora a videotape of one of the Globadine Ministries church services featuring Ron Mann. Because she had received a small life insurance settlement after the death of her husband, Nora had some money to invest. After seeing the videotape and hearing stories about members of her own church investing in the Faith Promise Plan and receiving money back, she decided this was an answer to her prayers.

"I had been praying for a miracle and this seemed to be it," she recalls. "I could increase my investment income and serve the church at the same time." So Nora started out investing a small amount in the program—$1,500—to see if it would work. But then she was shown additional tapes and heard other stories about people investing larger amounts and getting larger amounts in return. Let's pick up on Ron Mann's pitch.

> Mann: Now how many are tired of messing with small chicken feed? How many ready to go to higher stuff? Okay. I got a couple who raised their hands, alright.
>
> Let's say that you put in $61,000. Oh brother Mann, what happened to $50 to $250? Well it works the same way if you put $61,000 in, except you get more money when you put more in. How many know the more you sow, the more you reap? Everybody say that—the more I sow, the more I reap. Repeat this with me—say this like I said—Luke 6:38—"Give and it shall be given to me." Shakin up, running over, shall he cause men to give unto my bosom. Whatever I measure unto him, he will mete it back to me. Plus gas money to do it with. Amen?

Mann pours on the ether—only here it is a shrewd mixture of religious faith and greed. The reference to gas money is ironic because prosecutors later discovered that Globadine had dozens of so-called volunteers who would sell the Faith Promise Program and receive a 5 percent commission for any such gifts they brought in. The commissions were called gas money. Let's keep listening.

> Mann: Now how many live that scripture here tonight? If you give, you shall receive. Pressed down, shaken up, and run over shall he cause men to give unto my bosom. And whatever I give to him, he's going to mete it back to me. How many know you can't beat God giving, can you? The more you give, the more you receive, the more you quit giving, the more you quit receiving. Amen. Is that scripture? Did you know that anybody can do that and get blessed, they don't have to be a Christian to give and receive. But if you are a sinner and you give and receive, you can't get healed and you can't get . . . amen! . . . the benefits of the promises that God gives his people. So in order to get all them things, you need to give your heart to God, give and receive abundantly, and how many know that when you have God in your heart, you can give cheerfully, can't you?

This kind of pitch, wrapped as it is so thoroughly in the language of faith, was all Nora needed to hear to invest more. And as was true for so many of the Globadine victims, Nora relied completely on the word of members of her congregation and the messages she saw on videotape. She never even met any of Globadines' volunteers who were selling the program. In the end, she gave Globadine Ministries a total of $42,000. "I just thought if I could double $1,500, why not double $42,000," said Nora.

This is a classic example of what the SEC refers to as affinity fraud: infiltrating an established group for the purpose of gaining the members' trust and then exploiting them.

Mann doesn't stop at suggesting people should be giving larger amounts. He wants them to give larger amounts and then regift it back to Globadine, just like one would reinvest a stock dividend.

Pioneers of Fraud: William J. Miller

Most everyone has heard of Charles Ponzi, whose name is synonymous with Ponzi scheme. But some 20 years before Ponzi ran his infamous scheme, William F. Miller was launching the Franklin Syndicate in Brooklyn, New York, which pioneered what is essentially the same rob-Peter-to-pay-Paul approach to investing.

Miller's operation started small in 1898, but quickly grew after he got the bright idea to offer 10 percent per week or 520 percent per year to anyone who would invest any amount with his Syndicate. It was never entirely clear what the Syndicate's business was, but no one seemed to care. All these hungry investors knew is that this was by far the best

520% Miller invented what is now referred to as the "Ponzi" scheme

return offered anywhere by anyone. And for a time, the scam was believable because Miller had so much money coming in that he could afford to actually pay 10 percent per week to investors.[2]

The money came in even faster once Miller purchased mailing lists of investors all over the country and started mailing circulars with the 10 percent per week offer. He also offered investors an additional 5 percent return on any money invested by people they would refer to the Syndicate. The business exploded.

It is believed that Miller had more than 20,000 investors by 1899 despite the Franklin Syndicate never investing a dime in Wall Street. All investors were paid from the proceeds of other investors, and as long as new money kept pouring in, all investors were paid. Miller is believed to have taken in millions of dollars before the scheme was discovered and he was convicted of fraud.

This was not only an early precursor to the scheme Ponzi would run 20 years later in Boston, but also to the massive mail fraud schemes that would emerge in the 1920s and continue to this day.

> Mann: Well, why go 16 months and make $61,000 when you could regift every month and make double everything you give? Say that you put in $61,000 and you got $6,000 the first month and you didn't need the money, you put $6,000 back, then you would have $67,000 in the program.

The genius of regifting of course is that if you are running a Ponzi scheme where the money is not being invested but redistributed, you have that much more of other people's money to redistribute. According to prosecutors, many of the faithful chose to regift some or all of their investment.

The Close

Because federal regulators had been scrutinizing Globadine Ministries by the time Mann gave this presentation in 1999, he felt the need to raise the objection that Globadine might be a cheat.

> Mann: Let me ask a question. How many have been in the program at least two years? Alright. How many has been in the program at least a year and a half? Nobody. How about a year? You've been in a year? Okay, the sister has been in a year. Sister, in that year, have we cheated you any money? You got your money? Alright. We haven't cheated her in that year—you've got what we promised you. What the Lord promised you. We don't promise you—the Lord does. The Lord promises to give back to you pressed down, shaken up, and run over. How many know the only guarantee we have is Luke 6:38—his guarantee. How many of you know if you can't stand on God's word, there's not much other for you to stand on.

Mann very cleverly asks one of the women in the audience who had been part of the Faith Promise Plan if she had been cheated out of any money. It is not clear whether this person was a plant who actually was part of the scam or not, but she didn't really need to be since in a Ponzi scheme, most everyone gets money sent to them when they first join. It is only when the whole thing inevitably

collapses that people lose money. He also makes it clear that the
· returns he is describing are not being promised by him or by
Globadine but by the Lord. It is as if he and Globadine are merely
conduits for God's promise.

Then Mann starts to allude to the growing tension between
Globadine and the government:

> Mann: How may realize that our privileges are being taken
> away? The church and state. The state keeps hollering to
> keep the church and state separate, but how many know
> they want to keep separate until it comes to your money.
> They want to get a hold of the church books and find out
> how much God's money is. But God spoke in the Bible and
> he said, "Render unto Caesar what is Caesar's and unto
> God what is God's." How many realize that the money we
> receive and bring in—this is God's money. It says, "In God
> We Trust" on it, don't it?

Finally, as a final part of the close, Mann invokes the religious
version of the take away or what some cons have called the indifference pitch.

> Mann: Now those of you who are not in the program, if you
> are skeptical and you are not sure, then please do not
> join. Please just take the information with you, go home.
> You know, some folks can hear from God in a split sec-
> ond, some it takes 21 days and nights to hear from God.
> How many know if you are spirit-filled, God can speak to
> you quickly in your heart if you belong in this program.
> If you don't belong in it, we're still friends and we're
> still Christians. So if you come tonight expecting us to per-
> suade you to join, we're not here to persuade you to join,
> we are here to introduce you to the program, let you know
> it's available. If you want to be blessed by Luke 6:38, join
> the program.

In a nutshell then, Mann is essentially saying that it doesn't matter to him if people join the program, but they probably won't be

blessed by God. No wonder so many of the faithful invested their money in the Faith Promise Plan.

More than 18,000 people invested in the Faith Promise Plan, giving $450 million to what they thought was a church. Once it was closed down, authorities found that Globadine had spent the money on lavish cars for their volunteers and elders, and millions went to pay gas money (commissions). Officials found that some Globadine salesmen like Ron Mann were making more than $150,000 a month from the 5 percent sales commission they were paid—that's a lot of gas money.

And most of the people who invested received less than 10 percent of their principal back. Nora received $5,000 dollars back from her $42,000 investment. She was devastated by this experience, which put her even further away from being able to provide for her kids: "I am a religious person and I really believed that this operation was a sign that God was going to help me through this terrible situation. It all just turned out to be a big Ponzi scheme."

Nora was typical of many victims who had relied on word of mouth from friends and family members. Almost none of these victims checked on Globadine Ministries to see if it was registered with the government or had a prior record of trouble. And in fact, even if they had checked and found out it was not licensed to sell securities, Globadine officials argued that they were not selling anything—they were merely accepting gifts to God in behalf of the church and regifting back to those who gave. Obviously, state and federal authorities and the court system disagreed.

Conclusion

In the end, Globadine Ministries filed bankruptcy and most of those who participated lost everything they put into it. Nora Anderson and all of the victims eventually realized that Globadine was nothing more than a Ponzi scheme. And it was a Ponzi scheme that followed the classic stages of fraud: front, drive, close. What was most insidious about it was that it exploited people's faith in the church, in each other, and, ultimately, in God.

Tips for Avoiding Ponzi Schemes

- Never make a buying decision when you are in a heightened emotional state (under the ether).
- Beware of investments sold by friends or members of a group to which you belong, especially if they are not registered with state or federal securities regulators.
- Before investing, investigate and fully understand what the company does to earn the return it is promising. If you don't know how the company makes its money, it may be a Ponzi scheme.
- Verify that the investment is registered with the Securities and Exchange Commission (SEC) or with your state securities regulator.
- Verify that the salesperson or broker is registered with FINRA and/or the state securities regulator.

CHAPTER

Exploiting Fear

The Gold Coin Scam

*People out there are fearful because the economy is in shambles,
people are losing 40 to 50 percent of the value of their stock
portfolios, their annuities are down, their retirement accounts
are down, they're hearing about the banks that have gone under.
And there are economists all saying the same thing. Are you safer
at the bank on the corner or are you safer with your money under
your bed?*

—Jeremy Shipman, pitching gold coins in 2009

The sale of precious metals is as old as the hills. But the modern-day gold coin business, especially the fraudulent variety, looks an awful lot like the fraud crimes we have been describing in this book. In this chapter, we profile an operation we will refer to as The Rare Gold Company (not its real name), which marketed the sale of numismatic coins primarily to older investors based on a single human emotion: fear. While many legitimate coin dealers offer products at a fair price and gold coins can be a perfectly legitimate and profitable investment, many companies are using the uncertain financial markets as a way to bilk thousands of unsuspecting consumers out of their retirement money.

Jeremy Shipman is a former salesman for The Rare Gold Company. And was he ever good. Within six months of working there, Jeremy was the top salesman, personally taking in more than $1 million a month in gold coin sales, mostly from older people. In an interview conducted while he was waiting to begin a three-year jail term for a telemarketing fraud conviction, Jeremy described the atmosphere inside The Rare Gold Company: "It reminded me of the movie *Boiler Room*, where you have 20 guys dressed in suits and ties and they were sitting around in small cubicles answering the thousands of phone calls coming in off the radio ads."

The Front

Jeremy says the company advertised primarily on Christian radio stations nationwide. Why Christian radio? "My take is that Christians are more trusting and more open to believing in the good nature of human beings, and they believe most people wouldn't take advantage of them," he said.

Shipman says the primary objective of the radio ads was to cast a broad net and attract people who were fearful that the economy was collapsing. And in 2009 when these ads were running, it was not difficult to find such people. "The phones were just constantly ringing and there were stacks and stacks and stacks of people that had called in. It was huge."

Jeremy was very familiar with the ads and infomercials the company put on the air because he actually appeared as an on-air talent, pitching fear and calamity: "On the infomercials, my job was to describe how I was an expert at helping my clients look at their overall financial picture. I talked about how many people really don't even want to open up their statements and look at their values because they are losing 40 to 50 percent of their entire portfolio. Some people don't even know what kind of vehicles they're in. I was there to help stir up fear in people."

Stirring up fear about an individual's financial future in 2009 was not a difficult thing to do with record unemployment and the imminent collapse of mega Wall Street firms like AIG. As Jeremy said, "People out there listening to these shows were already in fear because the economy was in shambles, people were losing all their money in their stock portfolios, the annuities that they had were down, their retirement accounts were down, they were hearing about the banks that have gone under. So there was already all this fear about what should we do and where do we put our money, how do we protect ourselves?"

Edna Jones was listening to her favorite Christian radio station one day when she heard a 20-minute infomercial sponsored by The Rare Gold Company. The show focused on the turmoil being experienced in the investment markets on Wall Street and the fear that had been generated by people losing huge amounts of value in their portfolios.

Edna's husband had died several years before and had handled all of the finances, so she was a novice at investing. "Before my husband died, I tried to get him to teach me what he had been doing with our investments, but he refused to go there," said Edna.

When he died about a year later, Edna was left with virtually no experience in investing, and she was worried by reports she had read in the newspaper about the volatility in the stock market where most of her investments were kept. So she called an 800 number to talk to one of The Rare Gold Company's financial advisors. She was under the impression from the radio show that they were offering free financial advice. What she got was something quite different.

"When you call into these gold companies, you're not talking to someone who's there to teach you about the different types of gold or how to protect yourself," said Jeremy. "You're speaking to someone who has been trained to instill fear about losing your money, find out where it all is and high pressure you into parting with that money."

The Drive

Edna spoke to just such a salesman. He told her all about how gold was going to increase in value and how it was the only vehicle she could rely on. Jeremy did the same thing. "As a salesman, I was trained to tell people we have a team of numismatists who can hand pick your portfolio for you to give you the best annual return, and we've been averaging about 30 percent a year on the return for your portfolio. I also told them that gold was at $1,200 and was headed to $1,500 according to Wall Street experts."

79

As Edna and all the victims of these gold scams find out eventually, comparing numismatic gold coins to the market price of gold is deceptive because the price of an ounce of gold that is traded is based on something called bullion—solid bars of pure gold—which is not the same as rare coins.

In Edna's case, the salesman was very convincing and persuaded her that she should put all of her money in gold. Jeremy said that although the radio ads suggested a diversified portfolio where only 15 to 20 percent of your assets should be in gold, the salesmen were trained to ask for it all. "The office manager told the salespeople, 'When the buyer says to me, "How much money should I invest?," I tell them they need to invest all of it because you need to protect all of it. It's not how much of your money do you want to invest; it's how much of your money do you want to protect?'"

Just like business opportunity and oil-and-gas con artists, the gold coin scammers are trained to qualify the victim by finding out how much liquid assets they have. It is a process they call *discovery*. And in Jeremy's case, he didn't stop at identifying liquid assets. He went after retirement accounts and money tied up in other vehicles like annuities that had penalties for early withdrawal.

The Close

"My specialty was liquidating assets from annuity accounts and 401k accounts," said Jeremy. "When the buyer asked about the 10 percent penalty for liquidating, I told them they needed to stop the bleeding. I told them they had already lost so much money as it is, why not take the 10 percent hit, why not protect yourself, why not put it into something that's going to give you the future that you have always wanted to have—something that will be there for your grandkids."

Edna became so convinced that she should make a major investment in gold that she agreed to make a list of all her investments and send it to The Rare Gold Company. What she didn't realize when the Federal Express driver came to pick up the list was that the receipt they had her sign committed her to invest her life savings of $190,000.

Within a week, the company actually started calling her invest-ment company trying to convince them that Edna had authorized the full liquidation of her assets. When the investment company called Edna to verify this, she said, "I didn't agree to that."

Jeremy says this is standard operating procedure. "I would tell the buyer they needed to fill out paperwork and either fax it back or we would have FedEx pick it up. Then they would have them go to the bank and wire the money. And we would build up the fact that using a bank wire was very secure by saying, 'When you wire funds over telephone lines, you are federally insured and protected for the amount of money that you wire. And since you filled out the paperwork, your shipment will be secured because your shipment will be shipped by the post office ground. We are bonded with the state attorney general and the U.S. Attorney General's office, so you're protected.'" Jeremy was pretty sure The Rare Gold Company was not bonded with the U.S. Attorney, especially since it was under investigation by the U.S. Attorney.

Once Edna complained to the company that she had not intended to authorize a $190,000 purchase, they agreed to lower the amount to $95,000. What is incredible about Edna's story and the way this company did business is that she never even saw a list of the coins she was buying *until they arrived*. This too was common practice. "What we told buyers we were sending was a shipping and account agreement that they needed to fill out so that their shipment of gold would be protected," said Jeremy. "What we really had them sign was a contract that bound them to the purchase. They didn't receive a list of what they actually purchased until their gold arrived."

Jeremy says that very few people actually demanded to see a list of the coins they were buying before they bought them. He specu-lated that the reason they didn't demand to see the list of coins was that they were afraid to look stupid or to look like they were ques-tioning the salesmen. Many of the investors were, like Edna, older and inexperienced at investing. Salespeople were trained to get off the phone with people who asked a lot of questions. "Maybe 1 in 30 would be in that category of asking a lot of questions and we would just get them off the line as fast as we could. The vast majority of people would do what we told them to do," said Jeremy.

Reed Waddell was a con man in the 1860s who invented the Gold Brick Scam

Pioneers of Fraud: Reed "Kid" Waddell

Reed "Kid" Waddell was born in 1860 and lived most of his life in New York City. Like many con men, Waddell was from a respectable and well-to-do family. And he always had money. Newspaper reports from the 1890s describe him as a refined-looking man with a slim, delicate build who looked younger than he was.[1] He was always fashionably dressed, with his clothes hand-tailored from Europe and he wore the finest jewelry money could buy.

Waddell is credited with inventing the infamous *gold brick* swindle. Molding a piece of lead about the size of a brick, he would have it gold plated. Then he would sink a solid plug of gold in the center of the lead brick. He would then travel to the midwest and approach wealthy farmers with a story about how he had purchased the brick for $10,000, but had fallen on hard times and needed to sell it for $4,000. He encouraged the victim to take the gold plug to a jeweler to authenticate that it was real gold. The test would pan out and the farmer would bite, thinking he was getting $10,000 worth of gold for $4,000. What made this story believable was that during the gold rush days of the 1850s and 1860s, there were many stories of people stumbling into fortunes with the discovery of gold and silver. Waddell simply pretended he had a gold brick and then he would convince them the opportunity was real.

Newspaper reports from the times reported hundreds of instances where rural farmers fell for the gold-brick scam. Waddell is believed to have earned around $250,000 (the equivalent of roughly $4 million today) between 1885 and 1895. He was murdered at the age of 35 by one of his fellow con men, Tom O'Brien, after Waddell refused to loan him money.

Ultimately, Edna did agree to purchase $95,000 worth of coins. But getting the company to actually send them to her was another story. "It took six months of phone calls and complaining for me to get all the coins," she said. Edna finally did receive all the coins all right, but she noticed that many of them were silver coins, not gold. She became suspicious that perhaps the coins were not worth as much as the company had described. So Edna decided to take the coins to a local coin shop and have them appraised. To her utter horror, the local coin dealer told her she had paid $95,000 for about $40,000 worth of coins. "That's when I decided it was fighting time," said Edna.

Jeremy says that part of the story is also very common. He says that the company took 30 percent off the top of the purchase price to pay salespeople like him and the sales manager. But even more shocking—he claims the company routinely marked up the coins by as much as 300 percent.

As Jeremy describes it: "The buyer doesn't realize that they paid $3,300 for a one-ounce Liberty coin, which is primarily the coin that is sold to buyers, and that coin has a real value of about $1,400."

According to Jeremy, when the buyer receives his or her coins, they are listed with prices next to them, but those prices reflect the 30 percent sales commission mark up and the 300 percent company mark up. Because most people don't really know how much gold coins are worth, they just assume that they paid the market price for them.

Edna was one of the lucky customers of this company. When she discovered that she had been taken, she hired a lawyer and after a two-year struggle that involved arbitration, intense negotiation, and expensive attorney fees, the company agreed to refund her money. It even agreed to pay her attorney fees.

"I got my money back alright, but it was a struggle," she said. "And at one point, the company told me the only way they would settle with me was if I agreed to never talk about the case publicly. I told them I wouldn't do that." Edna got her refund anyway and has learned her lesson. "The main lesson is never invest in something you don't understand," she said. "And never buy something without seeing it first and checking it out." Wise advise. And another piece of advice for anyone thinking about investing in gold coins? Shop for them at your local coin dealer and compare prices before deciding to buy.

And one last question for our former con man: Does he have any remorse for spending months ripping off older people? "I just feel very disgusted with myself, very ashamed at the person that

I became because I was telling people that I was helping them and the last thing that I was concerned with was their well being. I was just concerned with making a sale and making a commission and I would pretty much tell them whatever I was told to say, which I knew wasn't helping them at all."

Tips for Avoiding Gold Coin Fraud

- Never make a buying decision when you are in a heightened emotional state (under the ether).
- Shop around with local coin dealers for the best price on any particular coin you are considering purchasing.
- Never buy coins of any kind from a telemarketer.
- Never put an excessive amount of your investment portfolio into one type of vehicle like gold.
- If you buy gold or silver coins, take possession of them and store them in a safety deposit box—don't let the seller store them for you.

To find out more about how to avoid gold coin and other precious metal scams, log onto the Commodity Futures Trading Commission web site at www.cftc.gov/.

Exploiting Boredom

The Movie Scam

Have you seen the new Brad Pitt movie? It opened at $125 million.
How would you like to have a piece of that kind of money?
And maybe we can get you on the set—have you ever been to
Hollywood?
> —Bill Sullivan, former investment-fraud promoter

Allan Jennings spent his entire professional career as a chemistry professor at the University of California, San Diego. He and his wife raised a family in Del Mar, California, and in 1994, he retired happily, living on a modest state-employee pension.

Throughout his adult life, Allan invested minimally on his own, relying instead on regular withdrawals from his state paycheck into a defined benefit pension fund: "Every month, I would contribute to that fund and I'm glad I did, because it is essentially what I live on now. As a college professor, I never really made enough money to be a big investor."

But shortly after his retirement, things changed. His wife was injured in a work-related accident that left her paralyzed. After several years of legal wrangling, Allan and his wife received a settlement of $200,000 for the accident and Allan was, for the first time, in a position to be able to invest some money. He ended up investing largely in technology stocks.

"The tech stocks were going crazy and since I was a scientist, I figured I knew how to invest in technology. So I did that and I parlayed my $200,000 into $2.5 million over just a couple of years. The stocks were splitting every six months. I said, 'Wow, this is amazing. I'm a multi-millionaire.'"

And then the technology bubble burst in 1999 and Allan's $2.5 million shrunk to $12,000. Allan realized that he may have known when to buy, but he didn't know when to sell. As time went on, he and his wife continued to save so they could remodel their house to accommodate the wheelchair she was now forced to use because of the accident. Eventually, her disability got to be too much for both of them and she was moved to an assisted-living facility. Tragically, in 2003, Allan's wife died from an accidental overdose of medication administered by the facility. Allan was devastated by the loss, and the only comfort he gained was receiving an accidental death insurance payout of $300,000. "So it ended up that with all this accidental death stuff, I had quite a little bit of cash on hand," said Allan.

Within months of his wife passing away in 2003, Allan started getting calls from brokers trying to get him to invest in movie deals. He didn't know it at the time, but Allan was about to enter the dark world of telemarketing fraud.

Until his arrest and subsequent conviction for telemarketing fraud in 2009, Bill Sullivan ran fraudulent telemarketing boiler rooms like the ones that started calling Allan. During a 10-year period, Bill's boiler room operations took in more than $20 million from investors. While several low-cost family movies were actually produced, none made any money, and all of the investors lost everything they invested with Bill. He is currently serving a three-year sentence in a federal prison in California.

The Front

In an interview given just before he began his prison sentence, Bill described the kinds of movie-deal operations he ran. It turns out that fraudulent movie deals look an awful lot like the fraudulent business-opportunity and oil-and-gas deals described in previous chapters. Bill described how the front-drive-close stages of fraud were precisely how his scams operated.

> Bill: We would have a bunch of guys called fronters and they call between 200 and 250 people a day. Many of these guys bounce from room to room and had actually worked in oil-and-gas rooms before pitching movies. Once they get someone on the phone, they asked them a bunch of questions to qualify them. They would ask about previous investments, how much they are worth, and are they liquid for $25,000 to $50,000.

Allan Jennings was one of those investors. "I started getting a lot of calls after my wife died," he said. "I must have gotten on somebody's list. I was called a *qualified investor*—qualified for what I'm not sure."

Allan doesn't remember all the details of those first calls. But he does recall discussing his finances with the salesmen and how he got the money to invest. They knew he was a widower. "I remember telling the salesman that I had this money that was just sitting there in the bank and that I wanted to have some fun with it," said Allan.

Bill said that investors like Allan who have lost their spouses are particularly hot leads: "Investors are looking for something to entertain them and take their mind off of their troubles. When someone has just lost their spouse, their guard is down and they're opening up to you. They're telling you the size of their estate, what's happening with their money. They will tell you anything you need to know because they need a friend, they need someone to talk to."

Bill said in these situations, his job was to become the investor's best friend. "I would listen to them. I would talk to them. I would bond with them. I would build the trust. Because once I build the trust with them, they are pretty much going to go along with what we're selling them," he said.

Bill said during the first couple of phone calls, the salesperson would ask the investor about favorite movie stars so that he could try to find one that may be available.

"We typically would just throw out names like bragging rights to see where the client would get excited," said Bill. "If I have a client coming in saying he'll put a quarter of a million dollars in your movie if he can have lunch with Farrah Fawcett, you know, we're going to be on the phone trying to get the agent of Farrah Fawcett to ask if she will work for a couple days for $100,000."

In Allan's case, the salesman pitched him on a movie starring a famous actor who was one of Allan's favorites. The movie was completed and the salesmen told Allan that the first money in would go to pay back the investors and when the investors were paid in full, then any subsequent money would be divided 50/50 between the investors and the producers. He said Allan was guaranteed to make a three- to four-fold return on his investment.

The Drive

Promising such high returns on movie investments was plausible, according to Bill, because everyone knows there is so much money to be made in the entertainment business.

> Bill: I would always talk about whatever movie had just come out and how much money it made. "Did you see the new Brad Pitt movie? It opened at $125 million. How would you like to have a piece of that?" And then I would go into how that movie probably cost $70 to $80 million to make and they made $125 million in one weekend. Then I would tell the investor that all we are trying to do is make a movie for $3 to $4 million—we can't lose.

Allan said this is exactly what the salesman told him. "He pointed out that even in a recession, people still go to the movies, which is why the entertainment business is such a sure thing. And I remembered reading about big movies making $300 million dollars all the time and I thought, 'Well maybe I will get a million of that or something.'"

As part of the pitch, the salesmen sent Allan a packet that had a copy of the script. He liked it. "After I read the script, I said, 'You know, that's not a bad script. You put that in the hands of some good actors, it could work.'"

And since the salesman told Allan they had one of Allan's favorite actors lined up, it seemed like a sure thing. So they convinced Allan to give them $125,000 and they actually produced the movie and even sent him a special *executive producer* copy that he showed to his friends.

Bill said a key part of his pitch was promising investors that they could attend Hollywood premieres. "A lot of these investors live in the Midwest or in small towns and have never been to Hollywood," he said. "They have been very successful financially, but life has become kind of boring. So I would get them all excited by asking them, 'Have you ever been to a Hollywood premiere? You haven't? We have premieres for all our movies and all the stars come out.'"

The Close

Allan said the salesmen kept emphasizing that the great thing about movie investments is that you can make a lot of money, but also have fun at the same time, something that was particularly impor-tant to Allan in the wake of his wife's death. "I thought it would be fun to find out about the movie business and to pal around with some of these folks. You know, I was not so far from Hollywood liv-ing in San Diego. I thought it would be interesting." There was one claim these investment scammers made to Allan that came true: Meeting the star of the movie.

"They invited me up to Hollywood to go to the first public screening of the movie. While I was sitting there waiting for the movie to start, the star of the movie came in the side door of the the-atre and sat down right behind me. I thought, well—that's cool. That was part of the reward I was getting for being a part of that movie deal. That was fun for me."

The producers had told Allan that they were spending a lot of money on promotion and the movie was going to be opening in New York and Los Angeles to great fanfare. Allan was convinced he had made a good investment and that the movie was going to make him big money.

The Load

But about two weeks before the launch of the movie, the producers called Allan and said they urgently needed more money for a second production they were going to do. Allan suggested they wait until the first movie started paying off and take some of those proceeds for the second movie. The producers said, "We can't do it that way."

At that point, Allan made a decision he would later regret: "I thought at that point it was a slam dunk that we were going to make money on the first movie. So I took a $100,000 mortgage out on my house and sent them another $100,000. As it turned out, something went wrong with that first production—the marketing and distribution failed. The production company didn't know how to promote it and I never saw a dime."

Bill said that the key to ripping off investors in movie deals is the same key as oil and gas or real estate or any deal—strike while the iron is hot.

> A good closer knows he has 72 hours to keep you excited and get you to commit to invest. So you call them back as often as you possibly can while they are still excited and under the ether.

Bill had a number of ways he would close the investor. The takeaway was the most effective. "We would tell people who seemed to be hesitating, 'The movie business is not for everybody. We don't call everybody for this investment. You've been qualified for this investment and what we want to do is show it to you and if you're interested, then we'll do business and if not, no problem, we'll part friends.'"

Bill said the minute the investor feels threatened, he will walk away, so it's important to show some level of indifference. "The key is to get them to want to buy it more than you want to sell it. Once that happens, the tables turn," he said.

Over time, many more Hollywood movie producers called Allan and pitched him on deals involving the entertainment industry. In the end, Allan invested more than $800,000 in various deals, none of which have paid him a dime. When asked why, after so many failed deals, he didn't just hang up on the callers, he said "Well I should have, but these deals all happened in a short period of time before the previous deals were finished. I guess I was under their spell a little. My son says, 'Dad, just say sorry not interested and hang up. Don't be polite.'"

Bill said that the main problem with deals funded by private investors through telemarketers is the cost of fundraising: "I would say that when you are talking about money solicited over the phone for a movie deal, 50 percent of the investment goes to pay sales commissions and another 30 percent goes to overhead for the company. So only 20 percent goes to actually make the movie. This is why most of the movies don't make any money."

Sound familiar? This is very similar to the oil-and-gas scam we described in Chapter 4. And like the oil and gas deals, the irony is that the private placement memorandum—the contract investors sign on these movie deals—often fully discloses the cost breakdown. Bill explains:

> Our private placement memorandum always disclosed that 80 percent goes to the company, but you'd have to read it very carefully to see that. And besides, very few investors ever read it. In the 10 years I did this, I can count a half dozen people who have actually read the memorandums or talked to me about it.

Allan acknowledged that he paid very little attention to the paperwork: "I looked it over sure, but I can't say I read every word." Nor did Allan ever have an attorney or accountant look over the paperwork. Recall from Chapter 4 what Johnny Weber taught his boiler room salesmen: "Buyers are not readers and readers are not buyers." From a fraud-prevention standpoint, perhaps the corollary to this phrase should be "Readers are not victims and victims are not readers."

With so much money going to pay sales commissions and so little money going to actually produce movies, we asked Bill if investors' chances of making a lot of money wasn't about the same as playing the lottery. "I think you're better off investing in the lottery than you are investing in the movie business."

Tips for Avoiding Movie Scams

- Never make a buying decision when you are in a heightened emotional state (under the ether).
- Before investing in a movie deal, find out if the salesperson is registered with the your state securities regulator and/or with Financial Industry Regulatory Authority (FINRA).
- Before investing, find out if the investment itself is registered with the Securities and Exchange Commission (SEC) or your state securities regulator.
- Be especially cautious of an offer that was brought to you by a telemarketer.
- If the salesperson starts to promise returns in excess of normal market returns (i.e., 30 to 80 percent or more a year), do not continue the relationship.

Exploiting the American Dream

The Business Opportunity Scam

I love payphones, man. I'm going to teach you how to sell advertising on the side of your phones. . . . We're going to sell advertising to the taxicab companies, to the scumbag lawyer across the street from the courthouse, to the bail bondsman across the street from the jail.

—Joe Vertega, All American Pay Phones

We began Chapter 1 with a description of a boiler room called All American Pay Phones. This company took in more than $20 million dollars from individuals hoping to start their own private pay phone businesses before the Federal Trade Commission (FTC) closed them down in 2000. In this chapter, we will dive deeper into the seedy world of business-opportunity fraud and get a bird's eye view of exactly how these con artists manipulate their unsuspecting victims. We will hear more from Joe Vertega, thanks to undercover audio recordings made by federal investigators. In addition, we will see Jimmy Edwards reenact how he would revictimize buyers before they had even taken delivery of their first order of phones.

Most Business Opportunity Frauds Are Alike

As we mentioned in Chapter 1, in an age where everyone has either a cell phone or a smart phone, it seems inconceivable that investors would be willing to pay money to buy a private pay phone distributorship. But in the mid-1990s, the cell phone was not as pervasive as it is today and the idea of owning a pay phone and profiting from it was still a plausible business idea—an idea that caught the attention of con artists in South Florida. While we are drilling down on a particular kind of business opportunity—pay phones—both Jimmy Edwards and federal authorities say that the business-opportunity frauds that were rampant in south Florida during the 1990s and 2000s all employed the same basic stages and tactics. Therefore, to see inside the walls of one such business-opportunity fraud is to see inside of them all. If you are having trouble imagining anyone being interested in pay phone distributorships, just insert the words wireless Internet or Blackberry or smartphone.

The Front

Recall that the main task of the fronter is to cast a net for possible victims, hook the prospect with phantom riches, and qualify the money. The way All American cast its net was to run small blind ads in newspapers all over the country:

AT&T-MCI Payphone RTEs
Prime Sites 150K yr
Pot'l Lowest Prices

Hundreds of these weekly ads generated thousands of calls into the All American offices, where salespeople like Joe Vertega and Jimmy Edwards answered the call and began the fronting process—that is when they weren't shooting heroin or snorting crack cocaine. Unlike many boiler rooms where there are a group of people who do the front call and a separate group of closers who do the drive and the close, the All American salesmen did all three. "It was a front-drive-close pitch. We didn't have a separate department with fronters like some rooms. We did it all," recalled Jimmy.

The undercover tape excerpts that follow were taken from court documents filed as part of the FTC's case against All American in 2000. All names have been altered.

Joe Vertega started his pitch outlining why it is possible to make a lot of money owning private pay phones.

> Vertega: John, pay phones are a numbers game . . . it's been legal for a private individual like you and me to own a public pay phone since 1984 when the Bell monopoly was first broken up. However, according to our research, as of the end of last year, 1998, less than 15 percent of the 3.3 million pay phones across the United States were owned by private individuals. The fact is that most people still don't know that they can own their own phone.

This statement sets the context for how big the potential market for private pay phones might be. But then he gets specific about the earning potential.

> Vertega: You have three different sources of income: number one, coin revenue, which will be the bulk of your income in an average location. Number two, you're going to receive commissions on every single long-distance phone call made on your phone. And number three, you'll be compensated now for the 1 800 numbers dialed on your phone.

You will recall from Chapter 1 that Joe dangles phantom riches by guaranteeing income of $300 per phone per month and that the prospect would recover his entire investment in the first seven to nine months. But he knows that while everyone would like these kinds of returns, not everyone who calls a blind classified ad will have the cash to be able to invest. So it is important to qualify the money.

> Vertega: If I brought you in as entry level with seven of the new-generation smartphones, by the time you're up and operating, you're looking at approximately a $15,000 overall investment. Are you capable of dealing with that?

Once the prospect says he or she is in fact capable of making that kind of a cash investment, then Joe moves into the profiling part of the pitch.

Vertega: What type of business are you in?

Swanson: Well, right now I'm an assistant manager at Starbucks, it's a coffee company. I don't know if you have that down there. And I've been sort of wanting to get into my own business for a while. You know, be my own boss and make some more money, obviously. So that's sort of what I was looking for.

Vertega: All right. Well, you and I both know this is America. There's only one way to get ahead, you've got to work for yourself. As long as you work for someone else, I don't care what you're doing, all you're actually doing is paying their bills, okay.

This exchange shows how Joe begins to profile the prospect by finding out what motivates him. He finds out where he works and that he has aspirations to own his own business. He then immediately focuses in on that and reinforces the prospect's motivation by saying that working for yourself is the only way to go.

The Drive

Joe then moves into the drive. The drive consists of customizing the pitch to match the individual's personal needs, legitimizing the offer by employing paid-for references (singers), and turning up the ether by painting a picture of vast wealth and success.

Joe knows that the prospect works at Starbucks and has said he wants to own his own business and make extra income. So Joe customizes his message by reminding the prospect of how independent this offer can make him.

Vertega: If you get involved with us, you're going to be an independent. This is not a franchise. As an independent, John, obviously I can't force you to accept any locations and I don't want to. My job is to turn you into an independent vendor and I give myself four to five weeks to do it.

Joe gets to the end of his first contact with the prospect and tells him that he can't go any further until he has the paperwork in front of him. So the prospect agrees to pay $15 for the package to be delivered via Federal Express, at which point, they would have another conversation. But before hanging up the phone, Joe wants to make sure that the prospect is going to call back, so he offers him a reference.

> Vertega: Mr. Swanson, I strongly recommend to you that you make a phone call today. I'd like you to get a better perspective of how the location process works. I'd like you to speak to my primary locator personally, who's been in your backyard.

All throughout the drive, Joe has emphasized the importance of finding the right locations for the phones and how All American has the best locators in the business. Now he is going to connect him to one before he has even committed to investing. Joe gives him the name and phone number of Arlen Cunningham, who Vertega says owned his own locations company.

> Vertega: The man does pay phones only, no gum machines, no pinball, no snack and soda vending, strictly pay phones . . . He's the best in the country. I want you to pick his brain. Find out what he knows about your territory, what he's got available, how he operates. Get a better grip on the location process, which of course is critical to your success. So call him. It will make it easier for me to teach you what I need to tomorrow.

Joe has just introduced a key element in the fraud pitch— the third party reference. In this case, according to Jimmy, Arlen Cunningham was on All American's payroll and was compensated for every prospect he spoke to, separate and apart from whether they hired him as a locator. He doubled as both a locator and a reference, which is also fairly common in the fraud trade. "A lot of times, we would give the prospect more than one reference and insist that they call them all before the close," said Jimmy: "It makes it easier because the reference is going to praise the company and help move the pitch along."

97

As part of the investigation, Swanson contacted Cunningham as instructed and Cunningham talked to him just long enough to find out where he lived and then told him he would call back. This is also a common practice among locators because they want to work with the closer to find out where the prospect is in the process. Once he had spoken to the closer, Cunningham called back the prospect and the first thing he said to him was this:

> Cunningham: In the Rockville, Maryland, area where you live, we have 43 locations. I already looked it up because we spoke the other day. They are top quality. These are places that are doing $300 to $350 to $400 a month in net revenue.

In other words, Cunningham immediately pitched the deal. As the conversation continued, Cunningham explained that he charged $300 per site, but his company works with All American to guarantee a location that will bring in a minimum of $300 a month, or they will relocate it at no charge.

One of the sneaky things about the use of references is that often the reference will find out additional information about the customer for use in the close. Toward the end of the conversation, Cunningham asked the prospect, "Do you have the financing already for this, John, or are you going to be going for a loan?" The prospect tells him no, that he has the cash. This is information Cunningham will immediately convey to Joe before he goes for the close. He has essentially requalified the money.

Once he has Swanson back on the phone with the package in front of him, Joe continues to drive the prospect. He provides a lot of details about the phone equipment to establish himself as an expert. Once he has demonstrated his mastery of the industry, Joe begins to turn the ether back up by detailing the profit potential of the deal. The essence of his message is that this investment will get the prospect started on a business that is going to grow rapidly and without much effort.

> Vertega: We start with $329 per phone per month cash profit, so for seven phones, that's $2,303 per month. You're not driving a Ferrari yet. But how long did it take you? Six hours

all month to collect the coins? If you take $2,303 and divide by six, that's $383 per hour . . . not bad as a part-time gig.

Joe then starts to paint a picture of how Swanson can expand his business and how All American is going to help him.

> Vertega: After seven months, you've pulled in $16,121 and you're in the black. You call me and say, "Joe, I'm in the black, send me seven more phones." And All American matches you phone for phone. I send you 14 phones for the price of 7 and you have 24 months to pay them off . . . interest free.

He masterfully turns up the ether on the prospect by suggesting not only that he will get back 100 percent of his $15,000 initial investment within seven months, but that is just the beginning.

> Vertega: So you reorder seven phones, I send you 14, and now you have 21 phones working for you at $329 a month per phone. That's $6,909 a month cash profit on a route of 21 phones after seven months. But that's nothing. To show you where I want to take you, I want you to have no less than 50 telephones within 17 months, maximum.

Vertega pours on the ether.

> Vertega: If you are listening to me, this is not pie in the sky, John. This is not win-the-lottery BS, sir. This is what I do for a living okay? $6,909 income on 21 phones. Let's multiply that times seven months. Now you've been in business for 14 months and you have $48,363 in cash built up. This of course assumes you have the discipline to save that money. Within 14 months, you've got almost 50 grand cash built up.
> Did you tell me you're a single guy or a married guy? Single? Well stay that way, John. I mean that from my heart. You've got 50 grand. Take 25 grand and buy John Swanson a new car. Make yourself happy. Do something nice. But take the rest of it and reinvest. Order 13 phones from me and I will send you 26. Now you have 21 plus 26 is 47 phones times

99

$329 a month. That's $15,463 cash income per month using conservative national averages.

Pure ether. And it is customized ether. Notice the question he asks the prospect in the middle of this barrage about whether he is single or married. Once the prospect says he is single, he customizes the pitch and tells him to buy a car with half of his earnings. With the other half, he continues painting the picture of escalating wealth and expanding monthly cash flow.

> Vertega: It's all about numbers, and your growth potential is unlimited. There's nothing to hold you back. You're not sitting in some little town in the middle of Utah or something. Your growth potential is unlimited.

The Close

After two conversations and almost two hours on the phone, Joe finally is ready to close the prospect.

> Vertega: Let me ask you a couple of questions. Number one, can you see yourself doing something like this?

> Swanson: Oh, yeah.

> Vertega: Can you see yourself going to your phones and collecting your money and keeping the accounting and keeping your phones clean, developing relationships with these business owners? You can see yourself doing that?

> Swanson: Oh, absolutely yeah. I've been wanting to get into my own business.

> Vertega: You're an intelligent guy. I can hear it already. Number two, can you see yourself reinvesting the better portion of what these phones earn?

> Swanson: Oh, absolutely yeah. That's what I would want to do primarily with it, yeah, because I mean expansion is—if you're not expanding, you're not doing anything.

> Vertega: Would you like to get started?

Swanson: I'm seriously thinking about it. I just want to take a few days and look over the pamphlet a little more and then probably move forward with it. But one thing I was wondering is whether it would be possible for me to talk to two people or so that are in the field right now.

Vertega: Absolutely. Now these people don't work for us, so I have to swap desks and get on another screen here. The software is programmed so that these names will not come up again. That's the way the owners want it, because they don't want anyone getting bombarded. But they are willing to take a few calls so they will know why you are calling.

Let's see who is coming up here. I can't control where they are or who they are, my friend, I have no idea.

Joe gave him the names of two people he said were distributors who had been with the company for some time. And the claim that they didn't work for All American? According to Jimmy Edwards, these were two of the most reliable singers they had. "They were both on the payroll. But we had to make it look like they were just customers, otherwise their endorsement wouldn't have meant anything," he said.

In the end, this particular transaction went nowhere of course, because the whole point was to pretend to be interested in order to gather evidence. But with the exception of playing the take away, Joe's pitch pretty much included every element classically involved in the stages of fraud.

The Load

We don't have an undercover tape recording of All American salesmen loading a victim for a second batch of phones. But we do have the next best thing, which is Jimmy Edwards, a former All American closer who also spent time as a locator, describing how he did the load. He starts by providing some background:

Edwards: At one point, I was the manager of the locations department at All American. We told buyers that the best thing about our company was finding great locations for the machines. In reality, the locater is there to help the closer sell more product to the victim. Let's say the buyer is in Chicago. I go into my database and I find an area that has a bunch of check-cashing places, because people who use pay phones also use check-cashing places. Once I find a place that has a lot of foot traffic and is near where the victim lives, I call him.

Hey John, great news, are you familiar with Metro Check Cashing? Based on our state-of-the-art databases, I have everything I need to know about Metro Check Cashing. Here's the deal, John. I got on the phone and I was lucky enough to catch the actual owner of Metro, and let me tell you how it went. This guy was so excited about how he can now have a private phone or two or three in his private locations that's not a Ma Bell phone and actually get commissions based on how many calls are done on a monthly basis out of that phone, that he wants me to put together a corporate proposal for him in two days and get it out to him and he pretty much guaranteed me that I could have all of the locations.

Jimmy is planting the seed of an idea. As we discussed in Chapter 3, a key load strategy is to call the victim and describe a new, surprising development that could make everyone a lot of money. This preys on the entrepreneurial notion that the best way to make money is to exploit changing market conditions or rapidly emerging developments. It also has the effect of building excitement, leading to the onset of ether. Then Jimmy ramps up the urgency.

Edwards: So I gotta tell ya, John, I am really excited about this. The only thing is—I want you to understand something and please don't take this the wrong way—I know you started out with four phones but I have to be honest with you, I can't let these locations sit there empty while you get your feet underneath you and start to move forward.

The whole thing is this. Once the owner gets a sense of how successful he can be in having a piece of the action in each phone in each location, he's going to get real excited and he might start calling around, finding out ways to put his own phones in there and then we're going to drop the ball.

Jimmy builds urgency by describing how these prime locations are available now but not forever. He sets the stage for the take away but also for yet another surprising development.

> Edwards: You know what John, let me do this. Let me touch base with the operations manager at All American, he's a friend of mine, we fish together on the weekends once in a while. Let me take a stab as far as an opportunity maybe to getting you some extra phones where it is a good deal monetarily. If we could do that for you, is this something you might be interested in?

Jimmy Edwards the locater has now become Jimmy Edwards the closer and he ratchets up the ether and excitement on the buyer to set him up to buy more phones.

> Edwards: Let me see if I can sprinkle some pixie dust on this situation and get you off and running because you are looking at a gold mine of locations here. Alright, let me get to work and I'll call you back on your phone in the next two hours and we'll figure out if we have made any progress, okay?

With that, Jimmy would hang up and not call him back in two hours. In fact, he doesn't call him back all day. He waits for the victim to call *him* back. This is a strategy to let the victim work himself into a frenzy of ether. And then when the victim does call back, Jimmy says:

> Edwards: I was just about to call you John. I have some great news for you. I'm going to call Sandy the operations manager right now and tell him you're available. It just so happens, in a twist of fate, you have a hell of a situation. I can't really explain it, I'm going to let Sandy do that for you. I just hope to God that when you come out here to visit with me in six to eight months, that you take me on a nice fishing trip for the day and then we go and have a nice dinner at a restaurant and you shake my hand and you are very happy.

Pioneers of Fraud: Peter Lake

Peter Lake, also known as Grand Central Pete because he operated out of Grand Central Station in New York, was a master swindler in the 1880s whose primary expertise was the bunco steering game. Here's how he played.

Another swindler known as a bunco steerer would spot the victim, then approach him or her with the following ruse. "Hey, Charles Baker from Cincinnati—it's been a long time since I have seen you." The person would look startled and then inevitably say something like, "My name isn't Charles Baker, it's Fred Campbell from Evanston, Indiana." The steerer would apologize for the error, try to get as much additional identifying information from the person as possible, then quickly walk over to Grand Central Pete and share the information just gathered so Pete would be able to approach the victim with his real name and other personal details which would put the victim at ease.

Grand Central Pete was a *banco steerer* in New York City during the 1880s and got his name by working Grand Central Station

Pete would then proceed to lure the victim into a back-room *bunco den* by telling him he had just won a lot of money in the lottery and he was on his way to collect it. He would invite the victim to join him. When they got to the bunco den, several accomplices would greet them, pretending not to know Pete.

Pete would produce a lottery ticket and his accomplices would pay him an enormous amount of cash. Pete would then play several games of three-card monte and win each time, followed by the victim trying his hand at it and losing everything he entered with.[1]

According to New York Police Chief Thomas Byrnes, Grand Central Pete was arrested more than 50 times in numerous towns all over the country, but was only convicted once. The rest of the time, he would have one of his confederates pay the victim the money that he stole and the authorities would let him go.

Okay? So Sandy is going to call you in the next five minutes because he is right in the middle of something right now but I want you and him to talk ASAP.

Then the phone rings and it's Sandy the operations manager (another closer) and he describes the situation to the victim.

> Sandy: We have a customer near Youngstown, Ohio, who has been in business with All American for the last three and a half years, and he has 65 phones in operation. He's a heavy hitter, and he just purchased eight new phones. But most of his family is in Europe, and a close relative of his died and he has been out of the country for the last eight weeks. In the meantime, the phones right now are sitting in freight forwarding waiting for him to return. And I gotta tell you, I need to get rid of these phones and I would rather take a hit on them than turn around and fly them back here and have to ship them back out somewhere else.

Thus, the closer Sandy and the locations manager Jimmy Edwards, working in cahoots, have just hit the victim with a second new development. Not only is there a fantastic location urgently available, there are also phones available at a fraction of the original cost.

> Sandy: So today is your lucky day John and let me tell you why. You purchased your phones for $1,399. I am willing to let these phones go for $659 and lock you into that price for the rest of your time working with All American Pay Phones. You know what that means? Every time you want to expand your route phone by phone by phone—you can do so for $659. You can take delivery of these phones in four days because they are sitting right now in freight forwarding in Ohio. All I have to do is call my dispatcher and ship them out.
>
> Now from what I understand, Jim was telling me you have tremendous potential with the Metro Check Cashing locations, which I couldn't help but go into my database and take a look at. I gotta tell you, and excuse the French, it looks like a f—king gold mine, John.

Conclusion

This is what you are up against if you happen to stumble into one of these operations: Fast talking con artists with lots of tricks and contrived stories to convince you that paying for overpriced pay phones is a smart move. While the pitch seems crude on one level, it is highly nuanced on another. They use everything from detailed knowledge of the product to fake references posing as customers to reloaders posing as locators who call with exciting new developments. A person calling All American or any of these bogus business-opportunity scams had better bring their A game and have their antenna up and a strong refusal script in their back pocket—or else they will fall prey.

Tips for Avoiding Business-Opportunity Fraud

- Never make a buying decision when you are in a heightened emotional state (under the ether).
- Ask to see all paperwork before you invest, and independently verify that the company is registered or licensed to offer business opportunities.
- Ask to see information required by law:
  - The names, addresses, and telephone numbers of at least 10 previous purchasers who geographically are close to you.
  - The number and percent of previous purchasers who have made as much or more sales, income, or profits as the seller claims you can make.
  - An explanation of how the seller knows how much previous purchasers have made, and how any claims about sales, profits, or earnings have been calculated.
- Get the seller's promises in writing. If a seller balks at putting oral promises in writing, consider doing business with another firm.
- Consider getting professional advice. Ask a lawyer, accountant, or business advisor to read the disclosure document and proposed contract.

For detailed advice on checking out a business opportunity, go to the FTC web site: www.ftc.gov/bcp/edu/microsites/moneymatters/jobs-business-opportunities.shtml.

CHAPTER 9

Exploiting Hope

The Lottery Scam

The thing people have to realize is none of these lottery mailers are legitimate. We never entered anyone in a real lottery. It's called mail fraud.

—Rick Barnes, convicted lottery con man

Alice, Doris, and Myrtle each have something in common. All three of them were single parents who raised children alone, worked hard, and followed the rules. Alice was a secretary, Doris was a telephone operator, and Myrtle worked for a power company. All three of them managed to save money for retirement so they could remain independent and not rely on the government or anyone else to provide for them. In many ways, these three individuals embodied the independent can-do spirit that is the hallmark of American culture. But these three had another thing in common—as they got older and friends and relatives began to pass away, they found themselves isolated and devoid of the hope of ever having any excitement in their lives. All three lost their life savings to the lottery scam.

Alice—Age 75

Alice had been living alone for many years since her kids moved out of the house. But around the time she turned 75, she was finding it harder to get out of the house and felt increasingly isolated and depressed. One day, she received an unexpected call from a woman who informed her that she won second place in the Canadian lottery. The woman told her that since Alice was not a Canadian citizen, the winnings would not be turned over to her until she paid $5,000 in cash to cover her taxes. Alice was told to give the money to a "FedEx" driver who would come the following day to pick it up. She went to the bank and withdrew the money, all that she had in savings, and packaged it for the driver. The driver arrived wearing a FedEx cap, but the vehicle was not a FedEx truck. The driver explained that it was a busy delivery season and the vehicle he was given was not one in the regular FedEx fleet.

The next day, Alice received a second telephone call from the same woman who said that she had great news. Because the first prize winner was found to be ineligible, Alice was no longer the second place winner, but had moved up into first place. The caller asked Alice how she would spend the money. Alice said that she was a single parent who had raised four children and they never had an extra nickel. She told the woman that she would pay her children's mortgages and send the grandchildren to college. The woman shared Alice's joy and excitement and advised her to keep the winnings a secret to surprise the family.

The woman told her that the check would be delivered just like in the TV ads for the big national sweepstakes. It would be a big check, there would be balloons, champagne corks would pop, and "all of your neighbors will see how happy you are." There was just one matter that needed to be taken care of—she would receive her cash prize of double her previous award as soon as she paid the additional taxes, another $5,000. When Alice explained that she did not have any more money, the woman suggested she get a cash advance on her credit card, which Alice did. The same "FedEx" driver wearing the same cap and driving the same vehicle showed up to pick up the cash. Alice was so excited that she did not sleep that night.

Two days later, there had been no phone calls, no big check arrived in a balloon-filled van, and Alice eventually realized she was the victim of a scam.

Doris—Age 83

Doris spent 50 years working for the phone company in Seattle, Washington. She was a strong, independent woman who had raised a daughter on her own after her husband died at a young age. Despite being a widow for most of her adult life, Doris had managed to save a nest egg over the years for her retirement. Her daughter had gotten married and moved to Alaska, and Doris found herself living in a condo in north Seattle with no relatives nearby.

Then one day, at age 83, Doris received a letter saying she had won the Spanish lottery. All she had to do to collect her winnings was to send in a small processing fee. Doris was intrigued, so she sent $29.00 to a post office box. Within a couple of weeks, she started receiving more letters indicating she had won other lotteries and for a small fee and some paperwork, she could easily collect her winnings.

Within three months, Doris was receiving 20 to 30 pieces of mail a day and she was spending many hours laboriously filling out puzzles and registration cards with her phone number on them, and sending in hundreds of dollars. Then one day, she received a phone call from a man who said he was calling to inform Doris that she had won the Canadian lottery. "That's right," he said, "after all that effort filling out puzzles and sending in money," her ship had finally come in. He told her that all she had to do to collect the $2.2 million in winnings was to go down to her local wire-transfer company and wire $1,500 to pay the border tax and they would send her the winnings. Doris believed this person because she had just spent the past several months filling out cards and puzzles to win. In the weeks that followed, many more people called Doris and gave her some version of the same story. She kept spending money, but never received her winnings.

Over an 18-month period, Doris spent more than $150,000— her entire life savings—on various prize and lottery scam offers. All she had to show for it was an entire garage filled with small prizes and junk mail.

Myrtle—Age 79

Myrtle lived in Portland, Oregon, and like Alice and Doris, she too had worked her whole life to support her children as a single parent. When she got into her 70s, she began to get a little bored since her family had moved away and she didn't see her grandchildren as much as she had when they lived in town. One day, at age 79, she was looking through her mail and saw an offer to play the lottery. Myrtle had received these types of mailers in the past and thrown them away, assuming they were junk mail. But for some reason, this time she opened the letter and decided to send in the small fee of $10 and "see what happens." Within a week, she was getting four to five mailers a day from companies all over the country offering her different chances to win lotteries and sweepstakes. A common offer was that if she purchased a product from their catalogue, she could win a prize.

Like Doris, Myrtle began spending every day sorting through what was now an onslaught of mail—often 30 to 40 pieces a day coming in. Myrtle dutifully read every piece of mail and in many cases, responded with a small check. Then after several months, she started receiving phone calls from people claiming she had won a million-dollar prize and all she had to do was pay the $3,000 "border tax" or "processing fee." Myrtle sent in the money. "One man called and he had such a nice voice and—you know—really sold me on it. He asked me for $10,000 and like a fool I sent it," she said. In the end, Myrtle sent in $300,000—her entire life savings—and had to sell her house to have enough money to live.

Confessions of a Lottery Scammer

Are these three stories typical of lottery victims? Unfortunately, the answer is yes. While not all victims lose their life savings to this scam, many lose thousands of dollars and many of the victims are typically older women like Alice, Doris, and Myrtle.

Rick Barnes started out his career as a computer expert specializing in helping businesses reach customers through direct mailings. In the 1980s, when computers became more commonplace and most of his customers started doing direct mail on their own, he turned to the dark side of the direct mail business—creating fake lottery mailers claiming that you may have won the El Gordo or other foreign lotteries. While the amounts they asked for to play the foreign lottery were small—often only $6 to $8 at first, that was just the beginning. Once you said yes to one of these mailings, according to Rick, they would keep mailing you other offers and keep the mail coming until you either ran out of money or stopped.

For the next 20 years, Rick worked with an international group of con artists defrauding elderly Americans out of millions of dollars until his arrest by federal agents in 2007 for criminal fraud. He granted an interview to AARP in 2009 just prior to beginning his prison term to explain how lottery scams work.

Rick says that like most frauds, it starts with buying a lead list of individuals who have played the lottery or sweepstakes in the past. "To begin with, you go out to a list broker and you get names of people who have previously played lotteries, sweepstakes, contests. In the industry, we call them mooches: Someone who wants something for nothing," he said.

Rick says the key to the front in the lottery game is to start people out small with an offer that seems like they can't lose: "We would start by sending people a postcard that says if you mail back the cost of eight stamps, which at the time was only $3, we will mail you eight separate checks for $3 that you can play the lottery with. So initially, they think they are getting $24 worth of lottery money for $3. What we are really doing of course is qualifying the list. We are separating out people who are going to respond to this kind of stuff from people who don't."

All three of our victims—Alice, Doris, and Myrtle—talk about how their involvement with the lottery scam started out small and then got bigger. "I only sent in a small amount at first," said Doris. "It seemed like an innocent thing to do and it gave me something to look forward to."

Rick said when he was doing the lottery scam, they would mail out about 100,000 post cards with the stamp offer and 10,000 people would respond, which was a 10 percent response rate. Then they would immediately mail out a second piece to these same people, only using a different company name and address.

"It was easy to change the mailers, so we were constantly making up new company names and sending them out," said Rick. Table 9.1 shows a list of different company names on mailers that Doris

Table 9.1 Fraudulent Prize Offers Sent to One Victim from the Same Canadian Company

Date	Company	Winnings	Fee
10.12	Continental Reporting	$1.5 Million	$29.99
10.15	The Finance Department	$1.25 Million	$29.99
10.17	International Prize Reports	$1.2 Million	$29.95
10.18	International Prize Report Agency	$975,990	$19.95
10.20	International Prize Reports	$2.43 Million	$39.95
10.26	Grand Prize Awards	$1.0 Million	$19.95
10.26	Major Money and Awards	$2.63 Million	$39.95
10.27	Prize Assessment Bureau	$1.24 Million	$19.95
11.5	The Finance Department	$1.26 Million	$29.95
11.7	Grand Prize Awards	$1.00 Million	$19.95
11.17	Grand Prize Awards	$1.00 Million	$19.95
11.17	Continental Reporting	$1.5 Million	$29.95
11.26	International Prize Reports	$1.2 Million	$29.95
11.28	Prize Assessment Bureau	$1.24 Million	$29.95
12.8	International Prize Reports	$1.4 Million	$29.95

received over a seven-week period. Notice the numerous company names despite the fact that all of these mailers were sent from the same fraudulent business in Canada.

The second mailer would typically offer them the opportunity to join a pool of other lottery players for $20 that would give them a much better chance of winning. "We would tell them they would join a group of 100 other people and if anybody won, they would all share the winnings. And because we were talking about a lottery in Australia or the Netherlands, no one really knew if it was real or not. Of course, none of it was true. We just made it up," Rick said.

Rick says that in the second mailing, his response rate would double to 20 percent, which means that of the 10,000 people who responded to the first mailing, about 2,000 people would send in the $20 for the second mailing.

Rick said that sometimes they would actually send the victims a check in the mail for $3 to $5 and tell the people that was their share of the winnings. This would get them really excited, and most of the time the victims would take that $5 check, add some money, and play some more.

Myrtle claims that over the 18 months she participated with the lottery scam, she received a couple of small checks back from the companies. "It wasn't much, but it made me feel like what I was doing was real. I mean the check was good, too. I cashed it."

While Rick mailed back small checks to prime the pump and get victims to send in more cash, the more common ploy in the lottery game was to simply keep mailing offers with solicitations for money until the victims stopped sending checks.

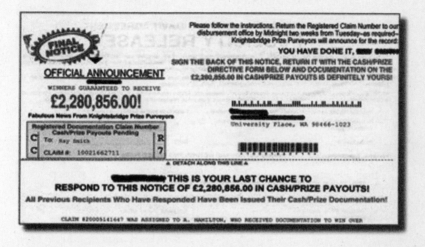

Sample fraudulent foreign lottery mailer

"We would mail to these people every 7 to 10 days until they stopped sending money. Most people played for six to eight months, and the average amount they lost was $500 to $600. The thing people have to realize is none of these are legitimate. We never entered anyone in a real lottery . . . it's called mail fraud," Rick said.

Myrtle and Doris said they were strongly persuaded to play the lottery when they saw pictures of previous winners in the mailings that were sent to their homes. "I saw all these nice pictures of happy people saying they had won the El Gordo or the Australian lottery, and I just thought 'it's my turn to win,'" said Doris.

Rick says that with modern computer technology, it is very easy to fake pictures of lottery winners. "We would take pictures of who knows who and we'd put them in the mailer and say, 'This is Edith Smith who just won $385,000 playing the Euro Pro Lottery with us.' Edith would give a little testimonial: 'You guys are great and made it so easy for me to win.' Of course, none of it was true. It's all made up—right out of our imaginations."

Pioneers of Fraud: Louis Gourdain

Louis Gourdain began his career as a clerk working for the Louisiana Lottery Corporation, a private company authorized by the state legislature in 1886 to sell lottery tickets nationwide. While there, Gourdain learned everything about the lottery trade, from printing tickets to direct mail marketing to watching millions of dollars roll in. The only trouble was Gourdain was only making $15 per week. So he quit and set up his own rival lottery (not authorized by the state) and modeled it after his former employer's operation, even calling it by the same name. He printed up millions of lottery tickets and mailed them in bulk to salesmen all over the country who sold them for a dollar per ticket, kept 20 percent, and sent the rest to Gourdain. He made $250,000 on this operation before being closed down by authorities.

Louis Gourdain started his own lottery scam in the 1870s and made millions of dollars before finally being convicted of fraud

Gourdain then ran several more fake lotteries over the next 20 years that reportedly netted him more than $2 million. Gourdain was prosecuted many times over his colorful career by attorneys general, postal authorities, and criminal prosecutors, but most of the time the charges were dropped because of a technicality or lack of evidence. When Gourdain was finally convicted of lottery fraud in a Chicago courtroom and sentenced to five years in prison, he told his attorneys not to appeal the case. They ignored him and got the case thrown out on a technicality. Gourdain was released from Joliet prison against his will. He then mounted a public campaign to have his sentence reinstated, which made headlines around the country.[1]

Gourdain was eventually admitted to a mental institution in Washington, D.C., after he threatened to pay back all his victims and then take his family out to sea and murder them. He escaped from the mental institution in 1908 and was never heard of again until word came of his death in London in 1913.

Rick says that with modern technology, it is even possible to download someone's picture from the Internet and alter it so that it no longer looks like the person. "You can steal somebody's face from anywhere and just modify it so it doesn't really look like them anymore. It's easy. A kid could do it—a teenager could do it at home."

One of the comments all three of our lottery victims made was that the letters they received must have been real because they were addressed directly to them. Each of the letters, they said, had their names sprinkled throughout the letter, which made them think someone had actually sat down and typed out the letter. Rick says that is simply another advantage the con man has with what is now basic, inexpensive software.

> You have a stack of names of people who have played the lottery before. Say you have 10,000 names. You simply take your letter and you draft it how you want it. And then all you have to do is put a one in this spot, a two in this spot, and you tell the computer to put the name where the one is, the address where the two is, and the zip code in the three spot.

Doris said the customized letters were what convinced her that the offers were real: "They even knew my birth date. If the whole thing was a scam, how would they have known that?" According to Rick, most of the time the victim herself gives you her birth date. "A lot of these astrology scams ask the victim for their birth date so they can tell them their future. Well, we buy the lead with that information and if you've got that, you can tailor the letter with it: 'Oh, you are a Pisces? That means you are going to win.'"

Rick admitted that most of the victims of lottery fraud are older people: "Your profile is definitely 50 and older. Most of them were shut-ins, people who didn't go out. They stayed at home and didn't have much to do. They go to the mailbox and say, 'Oh boy, I got some mail and it says I can win some money.' And they open it up and they don't got nothing to do, they'll read it, and they'll believe what they read and they go for it. Also, I think older people are the only ones who actually use the mail service. So they're the ones falling for it."

Tips for Avoiding Lottery Fraud

- Never make a buying decision when you are in a heightened emotional state (under the ether).
- Remember that all foreign lottery offers are illegal in the United States and most of them are frauds. If you receive a letter, e-mail, or phone call that you have won the Canadian or Australian lottery or the El Gordo, ignore it. It's probably a scam.
- If you know someone who says they may have won the lottery, counsel them to not send money for any reason.
- Keep in mind that modern technology makes it easy to create fake mailings with pictures of happy winners to prove the offer is legitimate. Don't fall for it.
- If someone offers to share lottery winnings with you, think about why anyone would do that.

10

Exploiting Credit

An Interview with an Identity Thief

In terms of how drug addicts get their money, ID theft has completely
replaced armed robberies, house burglaries, ATM holdups . . .
nobody wastes their time with that anymore.

—Sara Needleman

Identity theft—stealing someone's personal information and then applying for credit in that person's name—has become one of the fastest growing types of fraud in the United States. Fueled in the mid-1990s by the emergence of a deadly and addictive new drug, methamphetamine, identity theft went from a crime no one had ever heard of to the single hottest area of focus for law enforcement in the decade of the 2000s. According to the Federal Trade Commission (FTC), identity theft has held the top spot on the list of most reported frauds in the marketplace for 10 years (see Table 10.1).

Identity theft is different from other types of crime we have been describing in that most of the time it doesn't involve persuasion or a con artist pitching victims. Instead, the identity thief commits the crime by stealing a profile, which has basic identifying information such as Social Security Number, date of birth, and where you work.

117

Table 10.1 Top Five Complaints (Percent of Total)—FTC, 2009

Rank	2008		2009	
1.	ID Theft	26%	ID Theft	21%
2.	Debt Collection	9%	Debt Collection	9%
3.	Shop at Home/Catalog	4%	Internet Services	6%
4.	Internet Services	4%	Shop at Home/Catalog	6%
5.	Foreign Money Offers/ Counterfeit Checks	3%	Foreign Money Offers/ Counterfeit Checks	5%

Sara Needleman was a methamphetamine addict and identity thief for more than five years before finally being arrested by police in Vancouver, Washington. Law enforcement officials described her as one of the most elusive and clever identity thieves they had ever encountered because of her uncanny ability to move around, ship fraudulently acquired credit cards to vacant apartments and houses, and generally stay one step ahead of the heat.

Sara was in the identity-theft business long before law enforcement really understood the crime. In the past several years, many new anti-identify-theft laws have been put into place, and the business community has become acutely aware of just how big a threat it has become and is also taking precautions. Nevertheless, many of the tactics Sara employed are still being used today, and therefore getting inside the mind of an identity thief can be an effective way to avoid falling prey.

The Interview: Inside the Mind of an Identity Thief

Sara had been out of prison for about a year when she granted a single interview to AARP because, as she said, "My mother told me to talk to AARP." Brief clips of this interview appeared in an AARP documentary about identity theft, but the bulk of what Sara describes as an insider has never been made public. What follows is the complete interview that describes how she was able to steal identities and rack up credit charges of hundreds of thousands of dollars during her run as a prolific identity thief. At her peak, she had 17 people—mostly strung-out drug addicts—working for her at different levels of the operation—working as temps, dumpster diving, and mail-boxing.

How did you first get started in the identity-theft business?
"I first got into identity theft in the mid 1990s when the Internet was really starting to go strong and no one knew about ID theft yet. This also was when methamphetamine hit for the first time, and for some reason that really lit a fire under the identity theft stuff. Meth really took off because it was cheap, easy to get, and you could buy the ingredients at any grocery store.

"If there is a drug out there, I have tried it. I started with heroin and then I started cocaine, alcohol, you name it, I had tried it. And all throughout that time, I never once thought about doing crime. Then I started doing methamphetamine and boom—all these bad ideas started coming into my head. After being awake for 2, 3, 4 days in a row, you start becoming delusional. You start thinking of things that you normally just wouldn't think of. You start becoming paranoid, you start seeing shadows in the trees—they call them shadow monkeys. You would sit in your house and literally think things were coming by and they weren't there. And so to get my mind off of these bad things, I started thinking about crime. I was on the Internet and I just started thinking—boom—lightning flash—if I had this I could do that. It just all hit me.

"I remember seeing a site where it said 'instant credit card,' and I applied for it using a profile we had and got a $10,000 credit limit on a credit card. That's when it hit me how much money you could make. And law enforcement didn't really know what was going on at first because normal people don't think about this. It never occurred to the cops when we were first doing this that stealing personal information was the same as stealing actual cash from them . . . but it is. So that's why we got away with it for so long."

Is identity theft replacing other types of crime? "In terms of how drug addicts get their money, ID theft has completely replaced armed robberies, house burglaries, ATM holdups . . . nobody wastes their time with that anymore. The main reason is cameras and because you are going to get a lot more out of a profile than you are holding up someone at an ATM machine who is taking out $20 or $50 dollars."

What is a profile? "A profile is a set of information about a person that allows you to apply for credit in their name. A profile would have all the information we would need: name, address, date of birth, Social Security number, where they worked, previous address, in that order. We would pay people anywhere from $20 to $150 depending on how good the profile was, and we would make the people leave the profile with us so we could do a quick credit check on it first. There are a variety of ways to check to see what the person's credit limit is. If the credit limit was under $500, we would pay $20 for it. If it was over $1,000, we would pay $50. If it was 'we invite you to apply for a Platinum card,' we would pay $150 for it."

Who did you get to steal profiles? "The people I would hire to go steal profiles were drug addicts—and the dumber the better. I didn't want them to know what to do with the profiles, because if they knew what to do with it, I wasn't going to get it. So I would look for the person who was strung out the most, a person who would steal from their own mom, those were the things that I looked for. Because they are going to go out there and see the dollar, the dollar, the dollar—but the only dollar they know is the instant high . . . that's their dollar, unfortunately.

"So if I hired someone to steal five profiles and I gave them $20 per profile or $100, I knew that they were going to turn right around and give me back the $100 to buy meth with it. I would give them a deal and say if you get me $100 worth of profiles, I will give you $150 worth of meth. They would go for it every time."

What types of people have good profiles? "Older people definitely have better credit that younger people and the reason why is it wasn't as easy to get credit years ago—there wasn't as much out there. Younger people nowadays have 19 credit cards and I don't want that profile. They're already extended—their income-to-debt ratio is just insane. I want the person who has one Visa, one gas card, and that is a senior citizen."

Where would you send them to steal profiles? "There were three main ways we would profiles: mail-boxing, stealing from the workplace, and dumpster diving."

Mail-Boxing

"A mail-boxer is a drug addict we send out to steal mail from private mailboxes in residential communities. I really don't even want to say this because it's so bad, but . . . we targeted senior citizens. The best place to send a mail-boxer to is that place with the big sign on it that says 'retirement community—55 and older.' That's going to be your best hit by far. You already know first of all that everybody in there owns their own home because there are no rentals in there. Secondly, they are over 55 so they probably have a pretty good history with their credit.

"I would say that 80 percent of the profiles I used were senior citizens—if not senior citizens, then someone over the age of 45. Anybody younger than that, it was usually just a waste of our time. It's horrible but it's really true—they are the easiest victims out there. They have better credit, they have longer history at a job, they are on a pension plan, they have had the same bank forever, they are just plain and simple the best profile that's out there. Plus, they are the most trusting. They are the least likely to sit at home and think, 'Who could steal from me today?'

"So we sent mail-boxers out to all the retirement communities first. I would say we did it in two weeks. And then from there, we would go to what looked like the wealthier communities, but usually that was senior citizens also. If they weren't living in the retirement community, they were living in the wealthy community."

Does the gate around these communities slow the mail-boxer down? "The fact that a lot of these communities are gated, meaning they have a four-foot wall surrounding the houses, is not going to stop a mail-boxer. Because what is on the other side of that gate is so attractive: Your mailbox, usually together with a bunch of other mailboxes that all open with a single key. So the mail-boxer is jumping over a four- or eight-foot fence and they go right to your mailbox. They've got their bag, they are filling it up, they are throwing it over to the person waiting on the other side and they are jumping back over—the fence is nothing in terms of stopping these guys. And because all the mailboxes are there in one place, it's 10 minutes at the most. If you are there more than 10 minutes, you are leaving, you're not staying."

What is the easiest mailbox to steal from? The easiest mailbox to steal from of course is the old fashioned one that doesn't have a lock—you just open it right up and take mail out of it. The ones that people want to steal the most from are either in apartment complexes or suburban communities where access to the mail is from the back. There is a group of them—20 or 30 mailboxes in one spot that you can put a key into the back of, open, and all the mail falls out. That's definitely one of the best ones to get to.

"The best time to do mail boxing was between 12:30 AM and 1:30 AM. That was when the cops switched shifts and everyone else was asleep. Nobody was coming home from shift work—it was already too late—nobody was out walking their dog or anything.

"The mail-boxer is carrying those big green yard waste bags— it's got to be something cheap because you have to remember these guys don't have a lot of money, and I don't want to give them a lot of money because if I do, they will go get high with it instead of raiding mailboxes. They are all drug addicts."

Is it a good idea to put the red flag up when you have outgoing mail? "No, putting the red flag up is not a very good idea. I don't recommend that you put your outgoing mail in your mailbox and put the red flag up—that's just calling someone over to steal it. Thank you very much for telling us that you've got some money in your mailbox.

"Another thing to look for is if you go to the mailbox in the morning and there is mail all over the ground that was not because the mailman was clumsy. It's because your mail-boxer was clumsy."

Pioneers of Fraud: Walter Sheridan

Walter Sheridan was born in New Orleans around 1828. Newspaper reports describe him as well educated and a man of promise. Unfortunately, he got involved with the wrong element at an early age and by the time he was 30, he had been caught and convicted of robbing a hotel in Chicago, for which he served five years.

Upon his release, Sheridan got much more skillful at evading the law, primarily through his uncanny ability to assume false identities. He was variously known as Steward, John Holcomb, Charles Ralston, William Alexander, and Walter Stanton, among others. He was involved in so many different types of crime in the 1870s and 1880s that it is impossible to catalog them all. One newspaper account of Sheridan described him this way: "His history reads like a romance. His operations have extended to other countries and he is known as one of the shrewdest and most successful of the 'confidence men.'"

Walter Sheridan was a master con man in the 1880s whose specialty was assuming false identities and forging documents

Sheridan's biggest scam was the forgery of $100,000 worth of New York, Buffalo, and Erie bonds, from which he obtained a loan of $70,000. He was eventually charged with this crime and 80 other felony counts.[1]

Sheridan was an ingenious criminal, devising new and creative ways to commit otherwise-routine crimes like robbing banks. For example, he and his associates built a hollow walking cane that had a pair of tweezers on one end and a handle on the other connected by a spring that ran the length of the cane. Sheridan would walk into banks with the cane and appear to be perfectly innocent. But when the teller turned around, he would reach the cane across the desk and, with the tweezers, grab bank rolls that were out of reach.

Sheridan died in 1890, and when his body was examined, apparently the coroner found two five-dollar bills hidden under the plate of his false teeth—one final stash for safe keeping in case he might need it in the afterlife.

Stealing Profiles from the Workplace

Apartment Complexes "My experience has been that managing apartment complexes is a great place to steal profiles. The reason I know is that I got started in the identity-theft business when I was working as an assistant manager for a company that managed a number of apartment complexes. People would have to fill out a credit application to rent an apartment and when I would do the credit check, I knew all their information there. I would just make photocopies of it and take it home."

Department Stores "Department stores take a lot of credit applications, and so that was a good place to send in temps. Because at the end of their shift, department store clerks get a bonus for every credit application that they take and that is approved. So they could be writing down all the credit information and taking it home. I would definitely send people in to work at department stores. The bigger the store is, the better. The higher quality the store is, the better. And the reason why is you are going to have a higher quality of people going in there and applying for the cards. And we would send people in there for one week or one day. In one day, you can get 50 card applications.

"When we would send people into the department stores, the best job they could get was the shredder job. This was where you would take the bag of documents that had been identified as having sensitive material in it to the shredder. Well, those were exactly the papers we were looking for. If it's going to be shredded, then you know that there is confidential information in it. They would just take a box cutter and cut the clip tie and take whatever they could and they would bring it back to me and I would pay them for it. It's scary. Paperless will be the only way to ever be secure."

Doctor's Offices "We would send people into temp companies and then they would work in doctors' offices. The reason we would go to doctors' offices is because senior citizens go to doctors' offices. People who have medical insurance go to doctors' offices.

People who have medical insurance usually have a pretty good job, better profile, quicker money.

"They would go in to work as copy clerks, people like that. What else do you need? Medical records and a copying machine. They want one copy of everything, you are making two and putting one copy under the copy machine. Then at night, you're going to go grab those copies and you're going to walk out the door. And you might go back the next day but probably not—it depends on how much you got."

Dumpster Diving

"The people we sent out to dumpster dive actually got a rush out of it. They actually enjoyed jumping into those dumpsters and dragging papers out of it and bringing them to you—it was like a little kid coming home to mom and saying, 'Look what I got? Look what I got.' They would bring it to us and a lot of times, the people would be in such a hurry to get high that they wouldn't even wait to see what they had. They would just take $20 dollars or $20 worth of methamphetamine and be out your door. And here I am with a garbage bag full of papers—I could get nothing, but usually I got a lot."

Do you have any remorse about the things you did and the people you hurt? "I know that the victims were hurt by it and it does upset me—it does haunt me—it does. The first six months I was incarcerated was a lot of thinking, a lot of remorse, a lot of 'Oh my God, how could I have done this?' When I agreed to make this video, I agreed to do it because I wanted to do something to protect the people from having this be done to them.

"Meth takes your conscience and puts it in the dumpster that you are diving into. It really does. I didn't even think about it. Not once did I even think about who I was hurting or what I was doing to somebody and you know what I think my little mechanism was? I never saw the person. I never saw their face. I never, ever thought of it as anything more than a piece of paper. And I would just think to myself—well, I am just hurting the company and the company has insurance. The person I am doing it to, they can get their credit fixed. It's not that easy though. But that is what I would mentally go through to make it was okay to do what I was doing."

Are you worried that you might go back to meth and to this life? "I worry every day about encountering meth. I could not tell you to this day what I would do if there was some meth sitting here on the table next to me. I imagine I would probably run and scream out of the room as fast as I could. Because if I were to do it, it would all be over with. Once on meth, I would go right back to this life."

Tips for Avoiding Identity Theft

- Limit the number of credit cards you have.
- Get a locking mailbox.
- Limit the personal information you carry in your purse or wallet.
- Shred all documents that have personal information on them.
- Before doing business with a company, ask specific questions about its privacy practices, including:
  - Do you sell my information to anybody?
  - How long do you keep my information in a paper file before shredding it?
  - Do you digitize that paper file?
  - Are you a paperless company?
  - Do you conduct criminal background checks on your employees, including temps?

PART III

HOW TO FIGHT FRAUD

CHAPTER

Who Are the Victims?

Know thyself.

—Socrates

Many of us read about people being scammed and think, "It couldn't happen to me. I'm too smart, right?" Wrong. Social scientists are learning that fraud vulnerability may be less about how smart you are and more about behavioral factors such as how often you expose yourself to the marketplace, or psychological factors such as how easily you get excited or whether you tend to make snap decisions based on emotion.

Intelligence alone simply does not explain why so many highly educated, clearly smart consumers are defrauded every day. This chapter will provide more details about the specific attributes and behaviors that can lead to victimization based on almost a decade of fraud research. Let's begin with a quiz that gauges your vulnerability to fraud.

The Fraud-Vulnerability Quiz

Answer each question by checking the box that corresponds to your answer. Don't think too much about it or worry if it is the right answer.

1. In the past 12 months, have you sent away for any free promotional material in response to a TV, radio, Internet, or newspaper ad?

   _____ Yes

   _____ No

2. In the past 12 months, have you entered your name in a drawing to win a free prize, gift, or trip?

   _____ Yes

   _____ No

3. In the past 12 months, have you attended a business-opportunity or investment seminar that offered a free meal or other incentive to listen to a presentation?

   _____ Yes

   _____ No

4. In the past 12 months, have you opened and read most of the mail you receive, including advertisements?

   _____ Yes

   _____ No

5. Are you signed up for the Do Not Call List?

   _____ Yes

   _____ No

6. Which of the following statements would interest you enough to want to hear more information about the offer (check all that apply)?

   _____ This company is registered with the Securities and Exchange Commission (SEC).

   _____ The lowest return you can make is 50 percent per year, and some investors have made 110 percent per year.

   _____ There is no way to lose on this offer—it is fully guaranteed.

_____ More than 10,000 people have purchased this product in the past 90 days.

_____ This company has a solid track record with the Better Business Bureau.

7. In the past 12 months, have you asked for references and personally checked those references before doing business with a company?

_____ Yes

_____ No

8. Have you ever spent money on any of the following (check all that apply):

_____ oil-and-gas investment

_____ blue-chip stocks

_____ lottery ticket

_____ an infomercial offer

_____ commodity futures like frozen orange juice, silver, or wheat

_____ a business opportunity

_____ gold coins

9. Which of the following statements is most true for you?

_____ I prefer safe investments with average returns

_____ I prefer riskier investments with higher-than-average returns

Please indicate whether you agree or disagree with the following two statements:

10. I do certain things that are bad for me, if they are fun.

_____ Agree

_____ Disagree

11. I often act without thinking through all the alternatives.

_____ Agree

_____ Disagree

12. My age is:

_____ Under 18

_____ 19 to 30

_____ 31 to 49

_____ 50 to 64

_____ 65 to 80

_____ 81 or older

How to Score Your Quiz

While this quiz does not claim to predict future victimization, it does reflect many of the fraud risk factors found by social science researchers over the years. The scoring key can be found in Appendix A. Each question has at least one answer choice that may result in a vulnerability point. The lowest score possible is zero. The highest score possible is 17 vulnerability points. Anyone who scored 0 to 5 points is likely to be at lower risk of victimization. Scores of 6 to 11 represent moderate risk, and a score of 12 points or more represents a higher risk of victimization.

What Factors Make Us Vulnerable?

Numerous studies have been conducted that compare the behavior and demographic characteristics of known fraud victims with the behavior and demographic characteristics of the general public to see how victims differ. While this research continues, there are several general conclusions that can be asserted about all victims, compared to the general public:

1. **Exposure to Sales Situations.** More victims expose themselves to sales situations;
2. **Interest in Persuasion.** Victims tend to show more interest in persuasion statements used by con artists;

3. **Lack of Prevention.** Fewer victims take steps to actively prevent fraud;
4. **Risk taking.** More victims take financial risks;
5. **Low Self-Control.** Victims may have lower self-control; and
6. **Age.** Victims tend to be older.

Exposure to Sales Situations

Multiple studies have shown that, compared to the general public, more victims of fraud tend to put themselves in sales situations. AARP's National Victim Profiling study included interviews with 723 fraud victims and 1,509 individuals from the general public. The data from this study showed that compared to the general public, more victims sent away for free promotional materials, entered drawings, attended free lunch seminars, and read all mail, including advertisements.[1]

During the course of numerous in-depth interviews with victims of various frauds, this pattern of exposing themselves to the marketplace was evident. Whether the motivation to do so was financial gain, getting a good deal, boredom, or just an enjoyable hobby, victims were more engaged in the marketplace than others were. This finding was true even when controlling for age and income.

Interest in Persuasion

Several years ago, researchers analyzed hundreds of undercover fraud tapes made by law enforcement and found that across all scams, a series of identifiable persuasion tactics were common to most fraud schemes. The most common tactics were phantom riches (you'll make a lot of money), source credibility (you can trust me), social consensus (everyone is doing it), scarcity (hurry, time is running out), comparison (you're getting a really good deal), and friendship (do this for me as your friend).[2]

More recent studies have taken these same persuasion statements and asked victims and the general public to describe their interest in them. Consistently, the victims of fraud showed more interest in persuasion statements used by con artists than the general public, even after having been victimized.[3] Researchers believe this interest makes investors and consumers highly vulnerable to fraud. This is why questions about interest in persuasion are included in the vulnerability quiz and why persuasion is now a major piece of the Outsmarting Investment Fraud curriculum being delivered around the country.

Lack of Prevention

The research has not only found that victims expose themselves to sales situations and are more interested in persuasion statements used by con artists, but they also take fewer affirmative steps to actively avoid being defrauded. Several studies have shown that victims are less likely to be signed up for the Do Not Call list that limits sales calls and they are less likely to check references of a business before buying from that business.

Risk-Taking

Researchers have found that the willingness to take risks is correlated with fraud victimization. Studies of investment-fraud victims in particular have shown that more known victims had previously invested in risky investment instruments like oil-and-gas options, penny stocks, and gold coins than the general public had.

Victims also report that they simply prefer taking greater risks to get greater returns than the general public does.[4] This correlation makes sense given that any fraudulent offer to invest will have characteristics of higher-risk offers that may be legitimate: higher-than-market returns, often not regulated by the government, an opportunity that requires a quick decision, and so on.

Low Self-Control

One of the most well-established theories in criminology is the correlation between low self-control and criminal behavior. People who commit crimes tend to have lower self-control than those who do not commit crimes. But newer research has explored whether crime victims and specifically fraud victims also tend to have less self-control than the general public. Preliminary research points in the direction that lower self-control correlates to exposure to fraud offers and may even correlate to victimization itself.[5] More research needs to be done in this area, but the preliminary findings are promising.

The idea that victims of fraud would have lower self-control than the general public makes sense. After all, remember that the con artist's primary strategy is to get the victim into a heightened emotional state so he or she will make a buying decision based on emotion and not facts. It stands to reason, then, that those who are prone to making impulsive decisions would be more likely to succumb to the con artist's ether and become a victim.

Age

One of the most hotly debated questions in the fraud research world is whether older people are disproportionately victimized compared to younger people. While there have been a number of studies that suggest older people are not disproportionately victimized,[6] other studies showed the average fraud victim's age to be between 54 and 69 years old.[7] Because researchers will never be able to randomly select from among the total universe of victims, we will likely never know for sure if older people are victimized more than young people. But since 2004, the FINRA Investor Education Foundation and AARP have conducted extensive interviews with more than 1,700 fraud victims (chosen based on the availability of lists, not age) and the vast majority of them were more than 50 years old, which tells us something about age as a vulnerability factor. And one simple explanation for this could be the answer famous bank robber Willie Sutton gave when asked why he robs banks: "That's where the money is." Individuals over age 50 control trillions of dollars in assets, and the scammers are acutely aware of this fact.

Summary of Risk Factors

In looking at all victims of consumer fraud, there are essentially six primary risk factors that make one vulnerable to fraud:

- Exposure to sales situations
- Interest in persuasion

- Lack of prevention
- Risk-taking
- Low self-control
- Age

Any one of these behaviors or risk factors, taken alone, may not result in victimization. But the more that apply to you, the greater your risk.

Specific Profiles

Now that we have described how all victims differ from the general public, it is time to dive in a little deeper and look at two specific types of fraud victims: investment and lottery fraud. Table 11.1 describes a number of the major studies conducted in recent years of these two types of victims. Most of these studies were done by social service and regulatory agencies such as AARP and FINRA, contracting with survey research companies. For this reason, they typically do not appear in the academic research literature.

Table 11.1 Major Studies Comparing Fraud Victims with the General Population

Study Sponsor, Date, and Name	Types of Subjects	Sample Size
AARP Foundation/DOJ (2003) Off the Hook: Reducing participation in telemarketing fraud.	General Population (45+) Lottery Victims Investment Victims	507 310 132
FINRA/WISE Senior Services (2006) Investor Fraud Study.	General Population (45+) Lottery Victims Investment Victims	160 80 80
AARP (2007) Stolen Futures: An AARP Washington survey of investors and victims.	General Population Investment Victims	257 125
FINRA Foundation (2007) National Risk Behavior Study.	General Population (45+) Investment Victims	464 101
AARP Foundation (2008) Profiling investment fraud victims: A national study of investors and victims of investment fraud.	General Population (45+) Investment Victims	150 150

The Profile of an Investment-Fraud Victim

Many studies have been done of investment-fraud victims because so much money is lost each year to this crime and because so many people are now on their own as investors, given the decline of traditional pensions. Every adult American is a potential investor, so it is very important to understand specifically what makes investors vulnerable to fraud. These studies have found that investment-fraud victims differ from the general population in four specific areas: demographics, education and financial literacy, openness/exposure to sales situations, and risk taking.

Demographic Differences

Investment victims are older. Across all investment fraud victims in these five studies, the average age was between 55 and 65 years old. The average age of a U.S. resident is 36.8 years of age.[8]

Investment victims are more likely to be men. In four of the five studies, more than 60 percent of investment-fraud victims were men, which is considerably higher than the general population. In one study, 80 percent of all victims were men.

Investment victims are wealthier. In three of the five studies, a significantly higher percentage of investment-fraud victims had incomes of more than $75,000 as compared to the general population. In two other studies, no differences were found.

Education and Financial Literacy

Investment victims are more financially literate. Two of the studies asked both the general population and victims a series of financial-literacy questions. In both studies, the investment-fraud victims scored significantly higher than the general population. This was surprising given the assumption that higher financial literacy would lead to increased inoculation from fraud. An important note: While victims outscored the general population on financial-literacy questions, both groups did poorly, answering fewer than 60 percent of the questions correctly.

Investment victims are often more educated. In two of the studies, investment-fraud victims had significantly higher levels of education than the general population. In one of those studies, 66 percent of investment-fraud victims had graduated from college or graduate school, compared to only 25 percent in the general population.[9] In three studies, there was no significant difference between victims and the general population.

Openness/Exposure to Sales Situations

Several measures of openness were explored in these surveys and key differences between victims and the general population were found:

Investment victims attend more free lunch seminars. In four of the surveys, subjects were asked if they had ever attended a free lunch seminar. In all four studies, significantly more investment-fraud victims had attended a free lunch seminar than the general population.

Investment victims listen to unknown callers and read mail. In four of the studies, participants were asked if they listened to sales pitches from unknown callers and read junk mail. In three of the four studies, significantly more investment-fraud victims listened to sales pitches and read junk mail when compared to the general population.

Investment victims are more interested in persuasion statements. In three of the studies, participants were given a series of statements known to be used by con artists and asked to rate their level of interest on a one-to-seven scale. Examples of these statements follow:
- The lowest return you could possibly get on this investment is 50 percent, but most investors are making upward of 110 percent annually.
- This investment has made hundreds of people extremely wealthy.
- There is no way to lose on this investment—it is fully secured.
- We only have three units left. If you don't buy today, you won't be able to get in on this investment opportunity.

In each study, investment-fraud victims showed a significantly higher interest in these con artists' statements than the general population.

High-Risk Investing

In two of the studies, questions were asked about risk taking and investing.

> **Investment victims prefer high-risk/high-reward investments.** Participants were asked if they preferred high-risk investments with high returns to lower-risk investments with lower returns. In both studies, significantly more investment fraud victims said they preferred higher-risk/higher-reward investments.
>
> **Investment victims own more high-risk investments.** Participants were asked if they had previously owned high-risk investments like penny stocks or oil-and-gas investments. In one study, significantly more investment-fraud victims said they had owned high-risk investments compared to the general population. The second study found no differences between the groups.

Checking the Background of Brokers and Investments

Finally, in four of the five studies, participants were asked if they had ever checked the backgrounds of their brokers before hiring them. They were also asked if they had ever checked to see if the investment was registered before investing. In all four studies, there was no significant difference between investment-fraud victims and the general population in the percentage that said they checked. But very few participants from either group reported that they had checked the background of the broker or the investment. The range was between 28 and 38 percent of subjects reporting they had checked. This is an important behavior to try to change, since a huge percentage of con artists are either unregistered or are selling unregistered investments.

Summary of the Investment Fraud Victim Profile

These investment fraud-profiling studies reveal some significant differences between victims and the general population in key areas. Table 11.2 summarizes these differences.

With regard to demographic characteristics, multiple studies have now shown that the victims of investment fraud are more likely to be men, married, wealthier, and more educated than the general public. This clear profile allows fraud-prevention practitioners to both target and customize their prevention messages to a relatively narrow segment of the population.

With regard to openness to sales pitches, multiple studies have documented that investment victims tend to be more open to hearing about new products and listening to sales pitches than the general public. They also continue to be more interested in persuasion statements used by con artists. These findings also have implications for prevention in that they suggest that investors should be taught more about persuasion and how con artists use various tactics to defraud.

Finally, profiling studies have found that investment-fraud victims take more risks than the general public does and are highly unlikely to check the background of the broker or the investment before investing. These two behaviors can significantly increase the chances

Table 11.2   Profile of Investment Victims

Profile Descriptor	Investment Victims
Gender	More likely to be male
Marital status	More likely to be married
Age	More likely to be 55 to 65
Education	More likely to have a college degree
Income	More likely to have income more than $75,000 per year
Financial literacy	More financially literate
Sales pitch interest	More interested in con artist persuasion and sales situations
Risk-takers	More willing to take financial risks

of being defrauded. As you will see in Chapter 13, several agencies have built educational programs that focus on addressing these issues.

The Profile of Lottery Victims

In Chapter 9, three lottery victims were profiled: Alice, Doris, and Myrtle. As it turns out, nationwide studies of lottery victims confirm that these three women were fairly typical of the overall lottery-victim population. The two studies that inform the lottery profile were "Off the Hook" (AARP, 2003) and the "Investor Fraud Study" (FINRA/WISE Senior Services, 2006). The surveys administered to lottery victims as part of these studies were the same instruments used in surveys reported previously in this chapter for investment victims. We have simply separated the results to more clearly describe each profile. Four main areas have emerged that make lottery victims distinct from the general public: demographic differences, openness or exposure to sales situations, negative life events, and cognitive impairment.

Demographic Differences

> **Lottery victims are more likely to be women.** In both studies, lottery victims were more likely to be female.

> **Lottery victims are much older.** In both studies, significantly more lottery victims were over the age of 75.

> **Lottery victims are more likely to be single.** In both studies, significantly more lottery victims were single.

> **Lottery victims have lower incomes.** In both studies, significantly more lottery victims had incomes below $30,000 per year.

> **Lottery victims are less financially literate.** In both studies, lottery victims were significantly less financially literate, answering less than a third of financial literacy questions correctly on the surveys.

Openness/Exposure to Sales Situations

Participants answered a series of questions about behaviors that might increase their exposure to sales situations.

Lottery victims attend more free-lunch seminars. Even though lottery victims tend to be considerably older and poorer than investment victims and the general population, in one survey they reported attending significantly more free-lunch seminars than the general public.

Lottery victims are more likely to listen to unsolicited callers and read junk mail. In both studies, lottery victims were significantly more likely to listen to someone calling their home on the telephone and more likely to read each piece of junk mail they receive.

Negative Life Events

Coping with negative life events can sometimes interfere with decision-making. The lottery victims and general population subjects were asked if they had experienced any negative life events. Lottery victims were significantly more likely to experience the following negative life events when compared to the general population.

- Difficulty with a condition that limited your physical ability
- Death of a spouse
- Difficulties feeling lonely
- Difficulty with a serious injury or illness in the family
- Negative change in finances
- Legal problems
- Concern/money for basic necessities

Cognitive Impairment

In 2009, the AARP Foundation sponsored a pilot study that involved sending highly trained geriatric social workers into the homes of elderly lottery victims to perform mental-status evaluations to determine potential levels of cognitive impairment. These geriatric social workers specialize in such in-home mental-status evaluations and conduct them in their day-to-day jobs.

They used a standard assessment tool known as the *St. Louis University Mental Status* in combination with a clock test (drawing a clock face at a particular time) and their own in-depth interviews.

The average age of these subjects was 77. Nearly three-quarters of the lottery victims interviewed were assessed as having mild or moderate cognitive impairment. A few individuals showed signs of severe cognitive impairment and about 20 percent showed no impairment.

Given the older age of lottery victims, one might assume such rates of cognitive impairment are normal. But recent national studies of cognitive impairment among elderly Americans found that only 21 percent of individuals between 71 and 79 years of age and 53 percent of those between 80 and 89 have cognitive impairment.[10] While the results cannot be directly compared to national estimates due to methodological differences, it appears that victims of lottery fraud may have more cognitive impairment than other individuals in their age cohort.

Summary of the Lottery Fraud Victim Profile

Table 11.3 summarizes the various differences found in the research between the general public and lottery victims. Lottery-fraud victims have a distinct demographic profile that is different from the general population: older, poorer, more likely to be single, and female. They are also more open to sales pitches and more of them read their junk mail than the general population. It is pretty easy to see how this segment of the population might fall for fraudulent lottery mailings that offer instant wealth without having to do much more than mail in a small check.

In addition, lottery victims have had more negative life experiences than the general public, which may be a key contributing

Table 11.3   Profile of Lottery Victims

Profile Descriptor	Lottery Victims
Gender	More likely to be female
Marital status	More likely to be single
Age	More likely to be over 75
Income	More likely to have income under $30,000
Financial Literacy	Less likely to be financially literate
Life situation	More likely to have experienced a negative life event

factor to their victimization. As many studies have shown, coping with negative life events can and often does consume enormous amounts of cognitive capacity, using up vital reserves that might otherwise be employed to sort legitimate from illegitimate offers. The fact that they are more likely to suffer from higher levels of cognitive impairment or decline further exacerbates their vulnerable status and susceptibility to fraud.

Conclusion

Over a decade of research of fraud victims has found key demographic differences between victims and the general public, such as age, income, and marital status. But perhaps the more surprising finding is that many of the biggest factors that impact vulnerability to fraud are things people can change—like exposing yourself to sales situations, reacting emotionally to an attractive sales offer, or failing to sign up for the Do Not Call list. This makes sense since the con artist's goal is to get the victim under the ether and then force a quick, emotion-based decision.

These findings beg the question of what steps consumers and investors can take to avoid becoming victims. That is the subject of the next chapter.

CHAPTER

Become a Fraud Fighter

The only thing necessary for the triumph of evil is for good men to do nothing.
—Edmund Burke, Irish Philosopher and Statesman

If you have read all the way through to this point in the book, you know pretty much everything the fraud experts know about scams:

- The con artist's central strategy (ether).
- The stages of fraud (front, drive, close, load).
- The con artist's persuasion tactics (phantom riches, source credibility, social consensus, scarcity, comparison, and friendship).
- How scammers combine these strategies and tactics to extract money from victims (case studies of exploitation).
- Behaviors that increase vulnerability (being exposed to sales situations, taking an interest in persuasion, avoiding active prevention steps, taking investment risks, and having low self-control).

This means you are almost ready to become a fraud fighter. The final piece of your training is to review some straightforward tips on how to help yourself and your friends and family avoid being scammed.

Protecting Yourself from Fraud

There are four prevention strategies to consider:

1. Learn how to spot fraud from a distance;
2. Limit your exposure to the marketplace;
3. Make buying decisions based on facts, not emotion; and
4. Take precautions for avoiding identity theft.

Learn How to Spot Fraud from a Distance

Social scientists have conducted experiments over many years that show if you can see a request coming from a distance, you are better able to control how you respond to it.[1] The same is true for resisting a fraud attempt. The better you are at identifying a fraud attempt from a distance, the more success you will have resisting it. The following warning signs may help you see fraud coming.

Fraud Warning Signs

1. **Hyping the offer to induce ether.** The caller or salesperson enthusiastically describes how much money you will make and what you might do with it, in an attempt to get you excited so you will make a quick buying decision.
2. **Asking lots of personal questions.** The scammer is asking you lots of question about your personal life: How many kids and grandkids do you have? Where do you work? How long have you lived where you live? This is done to build rapport and to profile you so he or she can customize the pitch.
3. **Telling you that you've won a prize—but must pay to receive it.** The scammer may say that you have won a million dollars, but you must first pay administrative fees or taxes before you can receive it. It is illegal for a sweepstakes offer to ask for payment.
4. **Warning you that if you don't pay right away, you'll lose the deal.** Often scam artists will create urgency by telling you the offer will expire soon.
5. **Failing to tell you where your donations will go.** The scammer refuses to tell you how much of the donation goes to the

actual charity versus to the person calling. Legitimate charities are required to tell you this if you ask.

6. **Telling you the offer is secret.** The con artist tells you that the offer is top secret and you shouldn't tell anyone about it. This is intended to keep the authorities and possibly wiser family members away.

7. **Providing no written information.** Scammers want to keep you from making an informed decision so will often claim there's no time to send written material.

8. **Using fear.** Scammers will tell you the economy is collapsing and so you should buy gold, or crime is on the rise so you should buy a security system. Fear is a great motivator, but it is also the quickest way to induce ether.

9. **Getting a foot in the door.** The seller offers free gifts such as a CD or DVD in return for your willingness to sit through a presentation or buy a product.

10. **Using bait and switch.** A sale item is suddenly sold out, but a much better item is available for more money.

Limit Your Exposure to the Marketplace

Research has shown that individuals who are more open to exposing themselves to sales situations are more likely to be victimized by fraud. Therefore, reducing your exposure to such situations can be an effective prevention strategy. Here are several ways to limit your exposure:

1. Sign up for the Do Not Call Registry. The National Do Not Call Registry can help reduce telemarketing calls to your home (see Appendix B, Fraud-Prevention Resource List). Once you sign up, businesses are required to remove your number from their calling lists within 31 days. There are some exceptions, such as businesses with which you have a relationship, charities, and political organizations.

2. Opt out of direct mail. Just as exposure to unsolicited phone calls is a fraud risk factor, so is exposure to unsolicited direct mail advertising. The Direct Marketing Association's (DMA) Mail Preference Service will enable you to opt out of direct mail marketing from many national companies. To register with DMA, go online to www.the-dma.org/consumers/cgi/offmailinglist/ or send a letter to Direct Marketing Association, Mail Preference Service, P.O. Box 643, Carmel, New York 10512.

3. Limit attendance at free lunch seminars. As we learned in Chapter 11, victims of fraud were more likely to attend free workshops or seminars that offered a free lunch or dinner in exchange for listening to a sales presentation. While there is nothing inherently wrong with participating in such promotions, they do place you in a situation in which there can be enormous psychological pressure to make a purchase that you may later regret. If you insist on attending such seminars, commit yourself to the rule that you will not make a buying decision for at least 24 hours, which gives you time to think it over away from the pressure of the sales situation.

4. Limit the free prize or sweepstakes drawings you enter. Entering free prize or sweepstakes drawings often gets your name added to lead lists that will increase the number of solicitations you receive through the mail, over the phone, and across the Internet. By limiting the number of such promotions you enter, you are also limiting your exposure to the marketplace and therefore to potential scams.

5. Reduce unnecessary telephone solicitations. Even in the age of social media, Internet, and smart phones, many con artists still contact consumers via landlines to pitch them. Several strategies can reduce the number of unnecessary telephone solicitations you receive.

- Get a non-published number so that fewer salespeople have access to you.
- Install an answering machine and Caller ID to screen calls.
- Reinforce the free Do Not Call Registry with a "no solicitation" recorded message. Callers would be informed that this party does not accept solicitations and, if they are a solicitor, to hang up and place the number on its do-not-call list.

- Sign up for call rejection services through some telephone companies. Call rejection allows a customer to create a list of phone numbers that will be blocked. The caller would receive a recorded message that this party will not accept the call. Check with your carrier for availability.
- Use the call curfew service. This was originally intended as a tool for parents who want to prevent children from making or receiving calls during study or bedtime hours. Signing up for call curfew limits a party's ability to send and accept calls except to a list of pre-approved numbers. Some victims who have large families have reported that the call curfew list can be too restrictive since it is limited to 20 numbers. Check with your carrier for availability.

6. Limit the number of Internet solicitations to which you respond. Internet scams abound, and it is impossible to be too cautious when responding to e-mail solicitations or pop-up offers that appear while you are shopping online. The general advice is to avoid responding to any solicitations you receive over the Internet from businesses or individuals with whom you have had no previous contact. For more comprehensive information about Internet scams, log onto the FTC web site at www.ftc.gov/bcp/menus/consumer/tech/privacy.shtm.

7. Develop a refusal script. Many consumers and investors find it difficult to discontinue interactions with a salesperson or possible scam artist because they have been taught to not be rude. The simplest way to deal with this is to develop a one- or two-sentence refusal script that you can put by the phone or use whenever you are in an uncomfortable sales situation. An example would be as follows: "I'm sorry. This is not a good time. Thank you for calling."

Make Buying Decisions Based on Facts, Not Emotion

As we have said repeatedly throughout this book, the con artists' central strategy is to get their victim into a heightened emotional state so he or she will make a poor buying decision. If you are asked to donate to a charity, to make an investment, or to buy a product or service, do not allow yourself to be rushed into saying yes. Below are some tips for how to steer clear of the ether when making a buying decision.

1. Never make a buying decision at the time of the sales pitch.   Every sales training course ever invented has a section that, at some point or another, instructs the salesperson to "strike while the iron is hot." In other words, salespeople are told that once they get the customer interested in the product, ask for the sale before the customer loses interest. This is all well and good if you are buying a toaster, but if you are contemplating investing $10,000 in a business opportunity or a timeshare, it is in your self-interest to wait for that initial burst of interest to subside so that you can make a logical, fact-based decision.

The best rule for avoiding making a decision while in a heightened emotional state is to always wait a minimum of 24 hours after hearing a sales pitch. This provides time for your emotions to subside and to check on the business and the offer. Most con artists will try to get you to make a snap decision by offering all kinds of incentives to "act now," such as "the first visit discount" or the "one day only" sale or the classic "we only have one left" scarcity appeal. The reality is that there is no deal out there that can't wait 24 hours while you engage the rational part of your brain to help in making the decision.

2. Get everything in writing and read it before proceeding. Another way to ensure that the thinking part of the brain is engaged in helping you make a buying decision is to have a personal rule that says you will get the offer in writing and read all of it before making a decision. You will recall Johnny Weber, the oil and gas con man who instructed his swindlers, "Buyers are not readers and readers are not buyers." Several other cons have said similar things. The person they want to pitch is someone who likes making impulsive decisions without spending a lot of time thinking through the decision. Therefore, the best way to avoid making such a mistake is to be conscious and deliberate and to give yourself permission to slow down. The more expensive the purchase, the slower you should go.

3. Identify persuasion tactics used in the pitch.
As we have tried to show in this book, con artists draw on the same persuasion tactics over and over again. So one way to pay attention to how a sales presentation is influencing you is to consciously look for the tactics we have been describing in this book when you are watching a sales presentation. The primary tactics to look for are:

- Phantom riches (you'll make a lot of money)
- Source credibility (you can trust me)
- Social consensus (everyone is doing it)
- Scarcity (hurry, time is running out)
- Comparison (you're getting a really good deal)
- Friendship (do this for me as your friend)

If you would like to practice identifying tactics commonly found in fraud, simply turn on your television and watch any infomercial or home shopping channel that is selling products. While these programs are not frauds, they do employ all of the tactics that have been described in this book, and you should be able to readily identify them from the comfort of your own home. It can actually be kind of a fun exercise and one that you can do together with family and friends.

4. Ask for and verify registration and licensing information before proceeding. When it comes to investment fraud, regulators report that up to 90 percent of the scam artists they prosecute are not registered to sell securities. Therefore, one way to reduce your chances of being defrauded is to have another personal rule: Invest with only brokers and investments that are registered with state or federal authorities.

With regard to other consumer transactions, asking the basic question about whether a business is licensed and then verifying that licensing status does not guarantee that you will avoid problems, but it will greatly reduce the chance that the offer is a scam.

5. Check the complaint history of the organization with an Internet consumer service or with the attorney general's office for your state or with another relevant government agency.
A number of consumer membership websites allow you to search

for the names of companies and then read what others' experiences have been with that company. This is often a good source of objective information about how the company performs. You might also want to check with the state attorney general's office or your state securities regulator.

Take Precautions to Avoid Identity Theft

Because identity theft has become one of the biggest fraud threats in the modern era, it is important to reiterate some of the tips we described in Chapter 10 regarding how to avoid victimization.

1. Protect your privacy. Any personal information that you share with a business is likely to be recorded and sold to someone who is willing to pay for it. While most users of this information are legitimate businesses, it is important to be cautious and protective of your personal information.

2. Lock your mailbox. Using a secure mailbox will help to prevent criminals from stealing mail containing important personal and financial information. Incoming mail can include statements for credit cards, bank accounts, and investments. Put all of your outgoing mail in post office collection boxes or at your local post office.

3. Shred your documents. Before discarding documents and forms that contain your personal or financial information, such as Social Security number, bank accounts, or credit card numbers, shred them. Rather than using a shredder that cuts documents into long strips, use a crosscut shredder. Shredders can be purchased at any office supply store.

4. Reduce the personal information you carry.

Credit Cards—Check what you are carrying in your purse or wallet. Do you need to carry more than one credit card on a regular basis? If not, remove extra cards to reduce the risk of someone getting a hold of the cards or the information on the cards. Copy the front and back of your credit cards and keep the copies in a safe place.

Social Security, Medicare, and insurance cards—Do not carry your Social Security card with you. In addition, unless you have a medical appointment, you do not need to have your original Medicare or insurance card. Instead make a copy of your card and cross off all but the last two numbers of your Social Security number from the copy. Put the copy into your wallet and keep the original in a safe place at home.

5. Check your credit reports. You can get three credit reports free every year, one from each of the three major credit-reporting agencies: Equifax, Experian, and TransUnion. You can request your free annual credit reports from all three companies online at www. annualcreditreport.com, by phone at 1-877-322-8228, or by mail to Annual Credit Report Request Service, P.O. Box 105281, Atlanta, Georgia 30348-5281.

Protecting Friends and Family from Fraud

In addition to protecting yourself from fraud, it is important to have a strategy for helping other people you care about who may be targets of scams. The first step is to determine if a friend or family member is being targeted by fraud. Here are some warning signs.

1. **The phone rings off the hook.** The person is inundated with calls seeking charitable donations or offering money-making opportunities. This is a clue that they have already spent money on such offers and are being re-targeted or loaded by scammers.
2. **You see lots of cheap new stuff around the house.** Items like watches, pens, and small appliances are often part of order-to-win scams.
3. **Payments or frequent withdrawals are made to unfamiliar companies.** These can show up as checks or money transfers.
4. **Your relative or friend engages in secretive behavior.** The person will not discuss their finances or the types of calls or mail he or she receives.
5. **They have financial troubles.** Watch for a sudden inability to pay for basic necessities or bills.

6. They demonstrate mood swings. The person experiences mood swings such as being excited one minute (when they think they may be winning a prize) and worried and anxious the next (when the prize doesn't show up or the nest egg starts to shrink).

Intervention Strategies

Once you suspect a friend or relative is being defrauded, here are some steps you can take to help.

Build trust. If the goal is to protect assets and to ensure financial security, you need to develop a climate of trust. If the warning signs are present and it appears a person is being targeted for fraud, reversing the situation will require that the victim feel that the person offering help is not judgmental, but is on the same side of the table.

Help navigate. Offer to help sort through the mail to see which of the solicitations could be legitimate. If several organizations list the same post office box, question whether that seems likely. Point out misspellings. Remind the individual that foreign lotteries are illegal for U.S. residents, and you know the individual to be honest and law abiding. Refer to many of several publications offered by the Federal Trade Commission (see Appendix B, Fraud-Prevention Resource List).

Turn fraud targets into fraud fighters. Engage the individual in activities that will change how they view scam attempts. Ask them to look through their own mail for things that might be a scam. This could potentially change the lens through which they view such solicitations. Instead of looking for why a scam mailer might be legitimate, they are now looking for why it may be a fraud. Since people tend to find what they are looking for, this reframing effort might help.

Find alternatives. Targeted individuals may actually enjoy conversations with telephone solicitors and get excited when the mail arrives. Sometimes victims will refuse to stop taking the calls because they enjoy receiving them.

Exciting announcements of huge cash prizes by charming individuals who keep the victim under the ether can be addictive. Search out other activities to fill time previously spent being wooed by scammers and completing contest forms.

Be patient. As with all behavior changes, accept that the process will take time. Acknowledge incremental steps and encourage continued progress.

Coping with Being a Victim

Despite learning to spot the signs of fraud and reducing exposure to sales situations, victimization can still occur. Unlike other forms of crime, consumer-fraud victims are often unwitting participants in their own downfall. Fraudulent transactions frequently mirror legitimate business transactions, making it hard at the outset to differentiate between a lousy deal and fraud. Victim involvement or compliance can run the gamut from no involvement, such as a victim of identity theft whose information was stolen from an online database, to individuals who repeatedly participate in fraudulent sweepstakes and lottery scams.

Some victims are embarrassed and terrified that if anyone learns what happened, they will lose their independence. A common concern reported by older victims is how to get help without their family, particularly their adult children, learning what happened. They fear if word gets out that mom or dad has taken the bait, someone will decide it's time to move them out of an independent living situation. Compounding worries of being exposed are scammers who tell victims that warnings from family members are motivated by greed or jealousy.

It is extremely important for loved ones and caregivers to be supportive while sorting out the details. You may remember Alice, the lottery victim in Chapter 9. When she told her children that she had lost everything to scammers, their responses were so harsh that she felt devastated and reported that she didn't know if she could go on. It was only when one of the children put his arm around her and said that this could have happened to anyone that she regained some hope.

While we might be tempted to say, "It's only money," for older people with little chance of recovering what they've lost, it's a lot more than money. It may mean the victim cannot afford to remain at home. It may mean not being able to enjoy hobbies or travel to visit the grandchildren. In the worst cases, the victim may no longer be able to afford necessities for daily living, keep a pet, or pay for healthcare needs and medications. The best thing to do is to first say, "I am sorry this happened to you," and then offer to help.

The next best thing to do is to encourage the person to report the loss. Help the victim collect his or her thoughts, any relevant paperwork, or whatever details are available. Depending on the type of fraud, you may want to call the non-emergency number for your local police department for information about where to make the report.

Because some types of fraud, such as identity theft, may keep the victim at risk for years to come, it's important to get a copy of any reports in case they are needed later as proof of loss. See the resource list in Appendix B for places to report fraud.

Avoiding Future Losses

One strategy to avoid future losses by a loved one may be to open a new credit card account that has a low credit limit that could be used for telephone or online purchases. Another strategy may be to add a trusted family member to a bank account to regularly review expenditures.

While age is not the only predictor of victimization, evidence shows that older individuals comprise a disproportionate percentage of certain types of fraud victims.[2] Sometimes dementia and other cognitive impairments that are more prevalent in older people play a role in fraud and financial exploitation, which accounts for 20 to 30 percent of all reported elder abuse. Fraud cases involving vulnerable adults may require involvement of medical professionals, financial advisors, law enforcement, and the courts.

Every state has protections and resources in place for individuals who meet the definition of a vulnerable adult. Family members who suspect financial exploitation can speak with the individual's medical provider to see if medication or illness may be affecting cognitive ability.

It may be advisable to see an elder law attorney to discuss options for best protecting the victim with the least infringement on personal independence. While powers of attorney are important, they can also be abused if in the wrong hands. Guardianship is a reasonable option but should be considered a last resort because guardianship proceedings can be costly and the individual involved loses many significant personal rights. For a list of services funded by the Administration on Aging, contact the eldercare locator listed in Appendix B.

Conclusion

While fraud is prevalent in the modern marketplace, a lot of resources can help you avoid falling prey to con artists. By reading the content of this book, you have already taken a big first step toward preserving your retirement assets and helping others preserve theirs. Further, by taking a few simple action steps to better spot and resist malicious solicitations, you can virtually eliminate your risk of being taken.

CHAPTER

Fraud Prevention
That Works

*The biggest advantage I have is the investors' belief that he can't be
taken.*

—Ed Joseph, veteran con man

As long as there has been a marketplace, there has been fraud
like the kind described in this book. Law enforcement agencies,
social service organizations, and private foundations have spent
millions of dollars trying to prevent people from being taken over
the years. But insights from the social sciences literature, especially
psychology, are changing the way prevention practitioners think
about fraud. This chapter will describe some of the challenges to
delivering fraud prevention and what social science can teach us
about how to overcome them. It will also put a spotlight on two programmatic efforts that have been successful in applying this knowledge in the field—efforts that have resulted in startling rates of
behavior change.

Psychological Barriers to Preventing Fraud

To really internalize and use a prevention message, consumers and
investors must first believe the message is relevant to them personally. This is especially true in the information age where we are

bombarded by thousands of messages daily. There are at least five psychological processes that may create barriers to consumers finding relevance in warning messages:

- The illusion of invulnerability (it won't happen to me)
- Psychological reactance (you're not my boss)
- Threats to self-esteem (I am not stupid)
- Hot-cold empathy gaps (I'm cool as a cucumber)
- Positivity (just give me the good news)

Illusion of Invulnerability (it won't happen to me)

Many years ago, health psychologists identified a phenomenon known as the "illusion of invulnerability."[1] This is the idea that "other people get cancer, but I don't." The illusion of invulnerability is a huge barrier to changing behavior, because if you think you will never get cancer, then you will never do anything to prevent it. The same problem exists in the fraud-prevention arena.[2] Surveys consistently show that a majority of the general public think they are above average at resisting high-pressure sales and fraud.[3] Much like attitudes about disease, consumers acknowledge that fraud exists, but think they are too smart to fall for it.

To overcome this barrier, practitioners must devise ways to demonstrate to their audiences that they can be taken. Some agencies have employed gotcha-style strategies where they trick the audience into falling for a scam and then proceed to offer prevention advice and tools. The U.S. Postal Inspection Service was one of the first agencies to try this. In 1995, it mailed out 200,000 postcards to consumers that said they had won one of five prizes and all they had to do to collect was to call a toll-free number. When they called, they got an answering machine that warned them about fraud. The most startling thing about this tactic was that 20 percent of the recipients (40,000 people) called the number! It's pretty hard to argue that such offers won't lure you in when they just did.

Other fraud-prevention programs have participants fill out self-assessment surveys that help people better understand their own vulnerability. Such surveys may help convince overly self-confident

160

consumers that they should at least listen to the prevention messages being offered.

Psychological Reactance (You're not my boss)

Human beings have a natural aversion to being told what to do. This is true for five-year-old kids who ignore mom's plea to eat their vegetables and for well-off investors being warned about fraud. Most people simply do not want their freedom constrained in any way, even if it means putting themselves at greater risk. Psychologists refer to this as *reactance*.[4] Think about your own experience. Have you ever had someone insist that you do something, and your reaction (partial form of the word reactance) is to go out of your way to do the opposite? Some people will do the opposite of what they are being told even if they want to do it—just to assert their freedom.

To address this barrier, some practitioners have taken a page out of the con artist's play book and employed the indifference tactic: "It doesn't matter to me if you buy this investment." The prevention application of this tactic would be, "It doesn't matter to me if you don't check out the background of a broker. But it's in your best interest to do so." Such an approach is counter-intuitive, in that most of us think the best way to get people's attention is to tell them that your information is the most important thing in the world and they would be crazy not to listen to it.

Threats to Self-Esteem (I am not stupid)

No one wants to think of themselves as stupid enough to fall for a fraud scheme. And so the very act of listening to and practicing prevention techniques is an implicit admission that one might be taken. To overcome this barrier, some practitioners have employed the do-it-for-a-friend approach. In other words, when presenting fraud information, don't address the crowd as though they need the information; rather, tell them how smart they are to have come to the workshop and that they are the least-likely victims. But, as the story goes, if you are not the most likely victim, then someone you know is: a friend, a neighbor, a family member. So workshop participants are instructed to listen to the content not to protect themselves, but to be able to warn others.

Hot-Cold Empathy Gap (I'm cool as a cucumber)

The hot-cold empathy gap is a variation of the illusion of invulnerability. As we described in Chapter 2, human beings are notoriously poor at predicting how heightened emotions impact their own behavior. Individuals who are in a hot or heightened emotional state don't realize how their cognitive functions are distorted, and individuals who are in a cold or non-heightened emotional state are unable to accurately predict how they might be affected in the future by aroused emotions.[5] Both of these phenomena greatly assist the con artist, whose central strategy is to get you under the ether.

The hot-cold empathy gap is also a deterrent to learning how to avoid such effects. If people think they can handle their own emotions, then there is no reason to take steps to improve that ability.

One way to address this barrier is to build curriculum that puts participants in a situation where their emotions are aroused and then ask them to make financial decisions. This would allow them to see how such aroused emotions impacted their behavior. Many social science experiments have demonstrated this phenomenon over the years in laboratory settings. It would be interesting to field test such efforts.

Positivity (Just give me the good news)

One of the most well-researched areas in psychology has to do with differences in how humans view positive and negative information as they age. For example, psychologists have shown that older people prefer to focus on positive events and emotions as they grow older much more than younger people—the so-called positivity effect.[6] This has been demonstrated repeatedly in lab experiments where younger and older people are shown positive and negative images and then asked to recall them. Younger people recall both positive and negative images at the same rate, whereas older people remember more of the positive images.

Scientists have also tested this on anticipation of loss and gain, so called *affective forecasting*. Younger and older people are asked to react to the possibility of gaining money versus losing money, and younger people get equally excited about both; older people get excited about gains, but show little emotion around the possibility of losing money. This emotional disinterest in the prospect of losing has even been revealed in brain scans by researchers at Stanford.[7]

You can begin to see the possible impact of these differences in motivation in the fraud arena. If you get excited about potential gains but are not particularly bothered by the prospect of losses, then why not take a chance on an oil well in Texas?

Positivity can also be a barrier to fraud prevention in that most fraud messages tend to be negative: Don't be fooled; watch out for lying, cheating con men; and so on. In contrast, the con artist calls an older person and always has good news: "You've just won a million dollars." Therefore, one of the challenges when trying to reach older persons with the message that they may be targets is to frame those messages in a positive light. So instead of saying that 13 percent of the U.S. population is defrauded, one could say that 87 percent of the U.S. population is not defrauded because they are really wise and alert—and we can help you be among them.

Cultural and Practical Barriers to Fraud Prevention

In addition to individual psychological barriers, there are also several cultural and practical barriers to preventing fraud: It's a just world (so if something bad happens, it must be your fault); behavior change is difficult (you can't teach an old dog new tricks); and scalability (how to reach a critical mass of people).

It's a Just World (So if something bad happens, it must be your fault)

The just-world theory refers to the strong need that people have to see the world as predictable and just, a place where people get what they deserve.[8] Thus, whenever people don't get what they deserve and their just-world view is threatened, there is a tendency to look to the victim's own behavior as the cause of the injustice: "The only reason this rape/drowning/disease happened is because the victim did something that caused it." So for example, juries have acquitted rapists because they were persuaded that the victim encouraged the crime by dressing provocatively. People hear about a young co-worker being diagnosed with cancer and may wonder what behaviors might have caused it.

The just-world hypothesis can be a barrier to preventing fraud if policy makers believe fraud victims were simply greedy and deserved what they got. After all, dangling the prospect of phantom wealth only works if the victim wants to get something for nothing. With all of the pressing social problems facing lawmakers, it is simply easier to assume that fraud only happens to those who somehow deserve it.

It is undeniable that on some level, greed is a factor in fraud crimes. But in a culture that preaches materialism and the accumulation of wealth, the quest for financial gain is a cultural norm. In this environment, the fact that an individual's desire for wealth contributed to being defrauded should not move prosecution and prevention of the crime down the list of policy priorities. Ultimately, widespread cheating and lying in the marketplace leads to an overall erosion of trust that threatens the very foundations of the economy.

Behavior Change Is Difficult (You can't teach an old dog new tricks)

There is no doubt that behavior change is difficult—but not impossible. Meta-studies in health literature have shown that somewhere between 5 and 9 percent of participants in health-promotion/disease-prevention programs change their behavior as a result of the program.[9] While these changes seem modest, they are nevertheless life changing for those who actually stop smoking, lose weight, or increase their physical activity.

Unfortunately, there have been several high-visibility behavior-change efforts that have failed. A recent example was the national youth anti-drug media campaign. The federal government spent $1.2 billion on this effort between 1998 and 2004. A GAO report found that the program had zero effect on teenage drug use.[10] While the conclusions of this study were hotly contested by the administration at the time, many policy-makers nevertheless look at these examples and assume that one such failure means that there are no behavior-change efforts worth the investment. In other words, they throw the baby out with the bath water. This is a mistake. As the fraud-prevention case studies that follow clearly show, if programs are grounded in social science research, well designed, and well tested, it is possible to achieve lasting and significant behavior change.

Scale (How to reach a critical mass of consumers)

A huge challenge for addressing fraud prevention is that since theoretically anyone can be defrauded, everyone must be reached with prevention programming. For many years, agencies and non-profits would develop one-size-fits-all prevention materials as if they could fly over a football arena (figuratively speaking) and drop 60,000 brochures out of an airplane, hoping that by reaching everyone, they would also reach the 10 to 15 percent who are actually going to be taken. This approach made sense at the time, because agencies did not know which 10 to 15 percent of the public was going to be taken.

If the profiling research outlined in Chapter 11 tells us anything at all, it is that while theoretically anyone can be taken, some are more likely to be taken than others. Victims share particular demographic, behavioral, and psychological characteristics that distinguish them from the general public.

The good news is that in this age of limited government resources, reaching every consumer in the United States with prevention materials is no longer necessary. It is now possible to target resources to those populations that are most at risk and customize messages to increase the chances of success.

Prevention That Works

Given the number of individual and cultural barriers to preventing fraud that exist, it may seem difficult if not impossible to design programmatic solutions to address this problem. What follows are descriptions of two model fraud-prevention programs that have been designed to overcome the psychological and cultural barriers we have been discussing in this chapter.

The Outsmarting Investment Fraud Program

Outsmarting Investment Fraud (OIF) is a 90-minute curriculum that was co-developed by the FINRA Investor Education Foundation and AARP to provide investors with tools that can help them resist fraud. The curriculum covers three main areas:

1. Understanding risk: information about risk factors associated with being a fraud victim;
2. Understanding persuasion: information about the most common persuasion tactics used by con artists to defraud victims; and
3. Understanding prevention: specific prevention techniques investors can employ to avoid being taken.

Understanding Risk

The understanding risk section tries to address the illusion of invulnerability by providing the audience with a risk-assessment quiz similar to the one in Chapter 11. The quiz contains questions that research has shown correlate most closely to being a fraud victim.[11]

Workshop participants take the quiz at the beginning of the workshop and then score their own tests. They are then shown a chart that reports where victims of fraud and the general public scored on the same quiz and whether they fall into the green (safe) zone, the yellow (caution) zone, or the red (danger) zone. Most workshop participants score somewhere in the yellow or red zone, which tells them they may be at risk. The point of leading with such an exercise is to open participants up to the idea that they may have some exposure to fraud risk.

Understanding Persuasion

The centerpiece of the OIF curriculum is teaching investors the persuasion techniques used by con artists. Numerous studies have shown that if an individual can see a persuasive attempt coming from a distance, he or she is better able to defend against it. As was mentioned previously, recent studies have shown that, compared to the general investor population, victims of investment fraud are less able to spot persuasion tactics used by con artists.[12]   The OIF workshop covers the six major persuasion tactics most commonly found in investment fraud schemes so that investors will be better equipped to spot malicious use of these tactics in the future.[13]

Workshop trainers spend a considerable amount of time giving examples of each of these persuasion tactics—both the legitimate business use of them as well as the fraudulent use of them. So for instance, in describing social consensus, which is the tactic of showing that everybody is doing it so it must be good, the workshop shows the McDonald's Golden Arches and the sign that says "billions and billions sold" as an example of the legitimate use of social consensus. If billions and billions of hamburgers have been sold, they must be good. Then a fraud example is provided showing an audio-tape of a con artist claiming that his or her company has sold thousands of units of the investment being marketed.

Once the persuasion tactics have been defined and described, the workshop participants are shown a video spoof of a home shopping type of program that contains all of the tactics operating simultaneously. They are asked to pair up and count as many persuasion tactics as they can identify in the three-minute clip. This is intended to give the audience practice at identifying persuasion in the marketplace so that they will be better able to see it coming from a distance. They are then given the assignment to invite a neighbor over some day to watch one of these infomercials and discuss the persuasion tactics they see.

Understanding Prevention

The final segment is prevention, providing three main tips: Reduce your exposure to sales pitches, learn to identify persuasion, and ask and check the registration status of the broker. These three steps seem simple, but very few people practice them.

Does the OIF Workshop Increase Resistance?

To test the effectiveness of the OIF workshop, a series of pilot experiments known as *response testing* were developed. The goal of these tests was to determine if individuals who experienced the workshop would be better able to resist future fraud attempts than a control group that did not experience the workshop.

To measure the resistance effects of the workshop, a total of 275 people were recruited to attend one of two workshops: 117 individuals signed up for the first workshop and 158 individuals signed up for the second workshop eight days later. Participants were recruited from the same geographic region and the two groups were similar in age, education, and gender.

The first group was trained and then three days later, a telemarketer called those who had been trained and those who had signed up for the second training but had not yet received it. The telemarketer was experienced in making high-pressure sales calls and had worked in fraudulent boiler rooms for several years. Using a pseudonym and fake company name, the telemarketer told participants he was taking a survey of selected investors' views about the high price of gas in the United States. He asked each participant if he could mail them a written survey about gas prices, along with some information about an oil-and-gas investment. This approach is commonly used by fraud operators and is known as a *foot in the door*[14] because once the target agrees to a seemingly benign first request (survey), he or she is recontacted and pitched to buy a fraudulent investment.

Any participants who agreed to receive the mailing were coded as having responded to the pitch; any participants who hung up or declined were coded as having resisted the pitch. The telemarketer was not told which participants had received the training and which participants had not. For security purposes, each call made was closely monitored and nothing was ever mailed to any participants.

Results

Of those who did not received the OIF training, 36 percent said yes to receiving the information. Of those who did receive the training, only 18 percent said yes to receiving the information. This represents a 50 percent reduction in responsiveness to a fraud pitch as a result of attending the OIF training (see Figure 13.1).[15]

This significant reduction in responsiveness to a fraud pitch represents a hopeful forward step in the fight against investment fraud. The fact that individuals who participated in this experiment

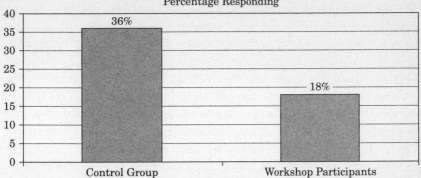

Figure 13.1 Behavior-Change Effects of OIF Workshop

were very similar demographically suggests that any change in response rate was likely due to exposure to the OIF workshop.

It is also worth noting that the foot-in-the-door tactic used by the telemarketer was not explicitly taught to those in the OIF workshop, yet they were able to use the persuasion training they did receive and apply it to a new tactic. This cross-situational use of the training is an important finding, since con artists continually change their pitches to reflect changing market conditions.[16]

The Fraud Fighter Call Centers

In Chapter 8, we profiled three victims of lottery fraud: Alice, Doris, and Myrtle. They are three of an estimated 3.2 million people in the United States who are victimized each year by fake offers to win a foreign lottery.[17] In Chapter 11, we described the emerging profile of the typical lottery victim: over 70 years of age, lower income, widowed or divorced, and less financially literate. Each year, the AARP Foundation's Fraud Fighter Call Centers contact hundreds of thousands of individuals who meet this profile and offer peer counseling to avoid future victimization. Regional call centers recruit and train hundreds of older volunteers who provide direct, customized fraud-prevention counseling to older adults on how to spot and avoid fraudulent offers. Older volunteers are recruited as fraud fighters because research has shown that receiving messages from a peer increases the effectiveness of that message.

Does peer counseling actually reduce fraud victimization?

In 2003, AARP and the U.S. Department of Justice completed a study of the call-center model. The study employed response testing and had professional telemarketers call lottery victims who had received a peer counseling call and those who had not and pitched them with a fake fraud offer. The result was a significant reduction in responsiveness to the pitch after a three-day delay.[18]

In 2010, Stanford University conducted a similar evaluation of the call-center model to measure its resistance effects over time. In a carefully designed study, more than 1,500 known lottery victims were identified and contacted through the call center program. Half of the group received peer counseling and the other half did not. Preliminary findings indicate that after a four-week delay, there was a statistically significant reduction in responsiveness to a fraud pitch by the group that received peer counseling (see Figure 13.2).[19] This is an important finding in that it shows that peer counseling can significantly increase individuals' resistance to fraud and that the resistance effect appears to persist over time.

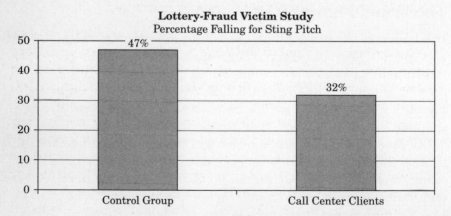

Lottery-Fraud Victim Study
Percentage Falling for Sting Pitch

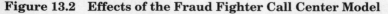

Figure 13.2   Effects of the Fraud Fighter Call Center Model

Conclusion

When it comes to fraud prevention, challenges getting through to consumers and investors persist. Too often, basic psychological factors get in the way of letting us hear and internalize messages that could save us from financial ruin. But prevention practitioners are learning how to develop programs that address these barriers, and there is growing evidence that these programs are working.

The Outsmarting Investment Fraud research project demonstrated that an educational curriculum can change behavior and help increase investors' resistance to investment fraud. And with millions of U.S. investors now responsible for their own financial security and struggling to cope with collapsing financial markets and burgeoning numbers of fraud operators, there is clearly significant demand for this kind of training.

The Fraud Fighter Call Center model has a track record of combining broad reach with proven behavior change. By recruiting and training hundreds of older peer counselors to contact vulnerable consumers with research-tested messages, the call centers are putting a dent in the fraud problem across the country. With fraud on the rise, an aging population, and vulnerable seniors responsible for their own financial futures, these call centers are, for many, the only thing standing between their money and ruthless con artists.

Call To Action: Join the Fraud Fighters

Your task, should you decide to accept it, is to embrace the ideas that have been presented in this book by social scientists, fraud prevention practitioners, and the scam artists themselves and use them to protect yourself and those people you care most about. Join the fight against fraud by sharing this book with friends, family members, and neighbors. Let them take the fraud vulnerability quiz, score it, and then have a discussion about why the questions they answered may matter in terms of their future exposure to fraud. Or organize a fraud-fighter reading group that periodically meets and discusses the latest scams identified in the marketplace.

Working together, we can put a serious dent in this devastating social problem.

The Fraud-Vulnerability Quiz

T he scoring key below will help you add up your score on the fraud-vulnerability quiz. Notice that some answers are worth 0 points and others are worth 1 point.

1. In the past 12 months, have you sent away for any free promotional material in response to a TV, radio, Internet, or newspaper ad?

   _____ Yes (Add 1 point)

   _____ No

2. In the past 12 months, have you entered your name in a drawing to win a free prize, gift, or trip?

   _____ Yes (Add 1 point)

   _____ No

3. In the past 12 months, have you attended a business-opportunity or investment seminar that offered a free meal or other incentive to listen to a presentation?

   _____ Yes (Add 1 point)

   _____ No

4. In the past 12 months, have you opened and read most of the mail you receive, including advertisements?

_____ Yes (Add 1 point)

_____ No

5. Are you signed up for the Do Not Call List?

_____ Yes

_____ No (Add 1 point)

6. Which of the following statements would interest you enough to want to hear more information about the offer (check all that apply)?

_____ This company is registered with the Securities and Exchange Commission (SEC).

_____ The lowest return you can make is 50 percent per year, and some investors have made 110 percent per year. (Add 1 point)

_____ There is no way to lose on this offer—it is fully guaranteed. (Add 1 point)

_____ More than 10,000 people have purchased this product in the past 90 days. (Add 1 point)

_____ This company has a solid track record with the Better Business Bureau.

7. In the past 12 months, have you asked for references and personally checked those references before doing business with a company?

_____ Yes

_____ No (Add 1 point)

8. Have you ever spent money on any of the following (check all that apply):

_____ Oil-and-gas investment (Add 1 point)

_____ blue-chip stocks

_____ lottery ticket

_____ an infomercial offer (Add 1 point)

_____ commodity futures like frozen orange juice, silver, or wheat (Add 1 point)

_____ a business opportunity

_____ gold coins (Add 1 point)

9. Which of the following statements is most true for you?

_____ I prefer safe investments with average returns

_____ I prefer riskier investments with higher-than-average returns (Add 1 point)

Please indicate whether you agree or disagree with the following statements:

10. I do certain things that are bad for me, if they are fun.

_____ Agree (Add 1 point)

_____ Disagree

11. I often act without thinking through all the alternatives.

_____ Agree (Add 1 point)

_____ Disagree

12. My age is:

_____ Under 18

_____ 19 to 30

_____ 31 to 49

_____ 50 to 64 (Add 1 point)

_____ 65 to 80 (Add 1 point)

_____ 81 or older (Add 1 point)

Scoring Key

0 to 5	Low fraud risk
6 to 11	Moderate fraud risk
12 to 17	High fraud risk

APPENDIX **B**

Fraud-Prevention Resource List

AARP—This nonprofit, nonpartisan organization has millions of members age 50 and older and provides information and resources, advocacy on legislative, consumer, and legal issues, and assist members in their communities. Go to www.aarp.org to find many resources in fraud prevention and consumer protection.

Annual Credit Report—You can request your free annual credit reports from all three companies (Equifax, Experian, and TransUnion) online, www.annualcreditreport.com; by phone at 1-877-322-8228; or by mail to Annual Credit Report Request Service, PO Box 105281, Atlanta, GA 30348-5281. This service is the *only* one authorized by law to provide you with a free credit report. Sometimes businesses such as your bank or insurance company may offer it as a service to customers. Other businesses provide a free copy only if you enroll in a separate for-fee service.

The Better Business Bureau (BBB)—This member organization works to resolve complaints between buyers and sellers, unless the complaint is one that falls under government regulations, such as discrimination. The BBB accepts complaints whether or not the business is a BBB-accredited business. You can find your local BBB by logging onto www.bbb.org.

Direct Marketing Association's (DMA) Mail Preference Service—This service will enable you to opt out of direct mail marketing from many national companies. To register with DMA, you can go online to www.the-dma.org/consumers/cgi/offmailinglist/ or you can send a letter to: Direct Marketing Association, Mail Preference Service, PO Box 643, Carmel, NY 10512.

Eldercare Locator—This is a service of the U.S. Administration on Aging to help identify resources for older persons in every community throughout the United States. Visit www.eldercare.gov or call 1-800-677-1116.

Equifax, Experian, and TransUnion—These are the three credit-reporting agencies. Another step you should take if you are a victim of identity theft is to place a fraud alert with the major credit agencies: You only need to call one of the companies and it will notify the others.

Equifax: 1-800-525-6285

Experian: 1-888-397-3742

TransUnion: 1-800-680-7289

Federal Trade Commission—If you are the victim of identity theft, you should file a police report and contact the Federal Trade Commission, which has a special clearinghouse for reports of identity theft. Call 1-877-ID-THEFT (438-4338) or go to www.ftc.gov/idtheft. The FTC also has excellent (and free) consumer education materials such as *Prize Offers: You Don't Have to Pay to Play!* You can contact the Federal Trade Commission at www.ftc.gov/ or call 1-877-FTC-HELP.

The Financial Industry Regulating Authority (FINRA)—FINRA is responsible for regulating all the securities firms in the United States. This is the place to check on individual brokers and to obtain investor-education information. Call 1-888-295-7422 or visit www.finra.org.

Fraud Research Center at Stanford—The Center seeks to facilitate our understanding, prevention, and detection of financial fraud by compiling information, connecting research to practical policy and fraud-fighting initiatives, and catalyzing research. The Center is a joint project of the Stanford Center on Longevity and the Financial Industry Regulatory Authority (FINRA) Investor Education Foundation. For more information, log onto www.fraudresearchcenter.org/.

Investor Protection Trust—IPT funded the Baylor College of Medicine in creation of *The Clinician's Pocket Guide* through its Elder

Investment Fraud and Financial Exploitation Program. Go to www .investorprotection.org

National Do Not Call Registry—Reduce telemarketing calls on your home and cell phones by calling 1-888-382-1222 from the phone you want to register. You can also sign up online at www .donotcall.gov. Businesses are required to remove your number from their calling lists within 31 days. There are some exceptions, such as businesses with which you have a relationship, charities, and political organizations. The number will remain in the registry until you ask to have it removed or you no longer have the number.

Office of the Attorney General—To file a complaint against a business, contact your state's attorney general's office. For a listing of the attorney general's office in your state, go to the National Association of Attorneys General web site at www.naag.org.

Opt out web site—Screened and preapproved credit applications can be a tool for fraud and identity theft. When these offers are delivered to the wrong address or stolen from your mailbox, they can be used by someone else to obtain credit in your name. Call toll free 1-888-5-OPTOUT (1-888-567-8688) or go online to www .optoutprescreen.com for details on how you can opt out of receiving such offers.

Secretary of State: Charities Division—To find out if a charitable organization is registered in your state, contact your Secretary of State's office. To find the web site or phone number for your Secretary of State, log on to the National Association of Secretaries of State web site at www.naag.org.

State Insurance Commissioner—Each state has an Office of the Insurance Commissioner that regulates all insurance companies. To find out how to contact your insurance commissioner, log on to the National Association of Insurance Commissioner's web site at www.naic.org.

State Securities Regulator—State securities regulators license brokers and investments and accept complaints from the public. You can find contact information for the agency in your state at the North American Securities Administrators Association web site www.nasaa.org.

Stop Fraud.gov—The site www.stopfraud.gov represents a network of 20 government agencies and 94 U.S. Attorney's offices and represents one-stop fraud reporting. There is a report fraud function that will take you to the various agencies and reporting forms related to the specific type of fraud.

U.S. Postal Inspection Service—The mission of the U.S. Postal Inspection Service is to protect the Postal Service and the American public from being victimized by fraudulent schemes where use of the mail is an essential part of the scheme. To file a complaint about suspected mail fraud call, call 1-877-876-2455 or log onto www.postalinspectors.uspis.gov/contactUs/filecomplaint.aspx.

U.S. Securities and Exchange Commission—If you want to check out a broker to see if he or she is registered, contact the U.S. Securities and Exchange Commission (SEC) at www.sec.gov.

Notes

Preface: The Big Myth about Fraud

1. K. Anderson, *Consumer fraud in the United States: The second FTC survey* (Washington DC: Federal Trade Commission, 2007).
2. K. Pak and D. Shadel *National Victim Profiling Study* (Washington DC: AARP Foundation, 2011).

Chapter 1   Inside the Con Artist's Mind

1. The name of the case file is being intentionally withheld in order to hide the true identity of the con men and victims involved.
2. Neal Shover, Glen S. Coffey, and Clinton R. Sanders, "Dialing for Dollars: Opportunities, Justifications, and Telemarketing Fraud," *Qualitative Sociology* 27 (2004), No.1, Spring.
3. *New York Times,* Lying to Suit Herself: Bertha Heyman making charges and contradicting them, January 24, 1883.
4. *New York Times,* Bertha Heyman's Pride: Don't care for money but does like to wrest it from her victims, July 11, 1883.
5. R. B. Cialdini, *Influence: Science and Practice* (Boston: Allyn & Bacon, 2009).

Chapter 2   Ether

1. AARP, *Telemarketing Fraud Victimization of Older Americans: An AARP Survey,* Washington DC (1996).
2. R. B. Zajonc, "Feeling and Thinking: Preferences need no inferences," *American Psychologist,* 35 (1980), No. 2: 151–171.
3. D. Goleman, *Emotional Intelligence: Why it can matter more than IQ* (New York: Bantam Books, 1995).
4. G. Loewenstein, "Out of Control: Visceral Influences on Behavior," *Organizational Behavior and Human Decision Processes,* 65 (1996), No.3, March: 272–292.
5. D. Goleman, *Emotional Intelligence.*
6. G. Loewenstein, "Hot-Cold Empathy Gaps and Medical Decision Making," *Health Psychology,* 24 (2005), No. 4 (suppl): S49–S56.
7. Ibid.

Notes

Chapter 3   The Stages of Fraud

1. A. R. Pratkanis and D. Shadel, *Weapons of Fraud: A source book for fraud fighters* (Seattle, Washington: AARP, 2005).
2. K. Pak and D. Shadel, "The Psychology of Consumer Fraud" (Doctoral Dissertation, Tilburg University, 2007).
3. A. R. Pratkanis and D. Shadel, *Weapons of Fraud.*
4. Thomas Byrnes (1886), *Professional Criminals of America* (New York: Chelsea House, 1969).
5. K. Pak and D. Shadel, "The Psychology of Consumer Fraud."
6. R. Thaler, "Toward a positive theory of consumer choice" *Journal of Economic Behavior and Organization,* 1 (1980): 39–60.
7. S. Milgram and J. Sabini, "On maintaining urban norms: A field experiment in the subway," in *Advances in Environmental Psychology: Volume 1: The Urban Environment,* ed. A. Baum, J. E. Singer (New Jersey: Lawrence Erlbaum Associates, 1978), 41–56.

Chapter 4   Exploiting Ego: The Oil-and-Gas Scam

1. J. M. Digman, "Personality structure: Emergence of the five-factor model" *Annual Review of Psychology,* 41 (1990): 417–444.

Chapter 5   Exploiting Faith: The Religious Ponzi Scam

1. The true case name is intentionally being withheld to hide the identity of the con men and victims involved.
2. *Le Mars Sentinel,* WF Miller: A Napoleon of Finance, December 11, 1899.

Chapter 6   Exploiting Fear: The Gold Coin Scam

1. *Mansfield News,* He Rolled in Wealth: Ill Gotten Gains of the Late Reed Waddell, May 1, 1895.

Chapter 8   Exploiting the American Dream

1. *Evening Gazette,* February 5, 1889.

Chapter 9   Exploiting Hope: The Lottery Scam

1. *The Des Moines Daily News,* July 22, 1906.

Chapter 10   Exploiting Credit: An Interview with an Identity Thief

1. *The Galveston Daily News,* October 10, 1884.

Notes

Chapter 11 Who Are the Victims?

1. K. Pak and D. Shadel, *National Victim Profiling Study* (Washington, DC: AARP Foundation, 2011).
2. K. Pak and D. Shadel, "The Psychology of Consumer Fraud."
3. K. Pak and D. Shadel, *National Victim Profiling Study.*
4. Financial Industry Regulatory Association (FINRA), *National Risk Behavior Study* (New York: FINRA Foundation and Applied Research & Consulting, 2011).
5. K. Holtfreter, M. D. Reisig, and T. C. Pratt, "Low Self-Control, Routine Activities, and Fraud Victimization," *Criminology*, 46 (2008), No. 1.
6. R. Titus and A. R. Gover, "Personal fraud: The victims and the scams," *Crime Prevention Studies*, 41 (2001), 54-77; K. Anderson, *Consumer fraud in the United States: The second FTC survey* (Washington DC: Federal Trade Commission, 2007).
7. K. Pak and D. Shadel, *National Victim Profiling Study;* FINRA *National Risk Behavior Study.*
8. United States Census Bureau, 2009.
9. AARP, *Off the hook: Reducing participation in telemarketing fraud* (Washington DC: U.S. Department of Justice, Office of Justice Programs and the AARP Foundation, 2003).
10. B. Plassman et al, "Prevalence of Cognitive Impairment without Dementia in the United States," *Annals of Internal Medicine*, 148 (2008), No. 6: 427–434.

Chapter 12 Become a Fraud Fighter

1. J. M. Quinn, and W. Wood, "Forewarnings of influence appeals: Inducing resistance and acceptance," in *Persuasion and Resistance*, eds. E. S. Knowles and J. A. Linn, (Mahwah, NJ: Lawrence Erlbaum Associates, 2004), 193–214.
2. K. Pak and D. Shadel, *National Victim Profiling Study.*

Chapter 13 Fraud Prevention That Works

1. L. S. Perloff and B. K. Fetzer, "Self-Other Judgments and Perceived Vulnerability to Victimization," *Journal of Personality and Social Psychology*, 50 (1986), No. 3: 502–510.
2. B. Sagarin, R. B. Cialdini, W. E. Rice, and S. B. Serna, "Dispelling the illusion of invulnerability: The motivations and mechanisms of resistance to persuasion,: *Journal of Personality and Social Psychology* 2002, 83, No. 3: 526–541.

3. FINRA, *National Risk Behavior Study.*

4. J. W. Brehm, *Responses to Loss of Freedom. A Theory of Psychological Reactance* (Morristown, N.J.: General Learning Corporation, 1972).

5. Loewenstein, "Hot-Cold Empathy Gaps and Medical Decision Making."

6. L. L. Carstensen and J. A. Mikels, "At the intersection of emotion and cognition: Aging and the positivity effect" *Current Directions in Psychological Science,* Vol. 14 (2005), 117–221.

7. G. R. Samanez-Larkin, S. E. B. Gibbs, K. Khanna, L. Nielsen, L. L. Carstensen, B. Knutson, "Anticipation of monetary gain but not loss in healthy older adults" *Nature Neuroscience,* 10 (2007), No. 6: 787–791.

8. M. J. Lerner, *The Belief in a Just World: A Fundamental Delusion* (New York: Plenum Press, 1980).

9. R. C. Hornik, *Public Health Communication: Evidence for Behavior Change* (New Jersey: Lawrence Erlbaum Associates, 2002).

10. GAO report to the Committee on Appropriations, U.S. Senate regarding the Office of National Drug Control Policy (ONDCP) National Youth Anti-Drug Media Campaign, August, 2006 www.gao.gov/new .items/d06818.pdf.

11. FINRA, *National Risk Behavior Study.*

12. K. Pak and D. Shadel, *Profiling Investment Fraud Victims: A National Study of Investors and Victims of Investment Fraud* (Washington DC: AARP, 2008).

13. A. R. Pratkanis and D. Shadel, *Weapons of Fraud.*

14. J. L. Freedman and S. C. Fraser, "Compliance without pressure: The foot-in-the-door technique." *Journal of Personality and Social Psychology,* 4, 196–202 (1966).

15. D. Shadel, K. Pak and J. Gannon, "The Effects of Investment Fraud Workshops on Future Investor Resistance," presentation at National Academy of Sciences meeting on Elder Mistreatment and Abuse and Financial Fraud, Washington DC, June 22, 2010.

16. Sagarin, Cialdini, Rice, and Serna, "Dispelling the illusion of invulnerability: The motivations and mechanisms of resistance to persuasion."

17. Anderson, Consumer fraud in the United States: The second FTC survey.

18. AARP, "Off the hook: Reducing participation in telemarketing fraud."

19. J. A. Menkin, S. Scheibe, D. Shadel, L. Ross, M. Deevy, and L. Carstensen, "Forewarned, forearmed? Effects of warning messages on rejection of fraudulent telemarketing pitches." Poster presentation at Gerontological Society of America Annual Meeting, New Orleans, LA. (November, 2010).

About the Author

Doug Shadel is the state director for AARP Washington and previously served as a fraud investigator and special assistant to the attorney general for the Washington State Attorney General's office. He is a nationally recognized expert on financial fraud, having co-directed numerous studies for AARP, the AARP Foundation, the FINRA Investor Education Foundation, and Stanford University. He has also co-authored several books including *Schemes and Scams* (with John T.), *Outsmart Crime* (with Al Ward), and *Weapons of Fraud* (with Anthony Pratkanis). In 2000, Shadel received the FBI Director's Award for his work fighting financial fraud. He has a Ph.D. in social science and lives in Seattle with his wife, Renee, and children, Nick and Emily.

Index

Index